To Dr. Hague,

How could I ever thank you for all the guidance, help, counsel and just good advice that you've given me over the last five years. I hope we remain friends forever.

Carrie Ethisco, Ph.D.

Reactions to the Persian Gulf War

Editorials in the Conflict Zone

Carrie Chrisco

University Press of America, Inc.
Lanham • New York • London

Copyright © 1995 by
University Press of America,® Inc.
4720 Boston Way
Lanham, Maryland 20706

3 Henrietta Street
London, WC2E 8LU England

Library of Congress Cataloging-in-Publication Data

Chrisco, Carrie.
Reactions to the Persian Gulf War : editorials in the conflict zone /
Carrie Chrisco.
p.   cm.
Includes bibliographical references and index.
1. Persian Gulf War, 1991--Press coverage--Middle East.   I.   Title.
DS7.739.C46   1995   956.7044'2--dc20   95-33259   CIP

ISBN 0-7618-0082-4 (cloth: alk ppr.)

⊖™The paper used in this publication meets the minimum
requirements of American National Standard for Information
Sciences—Permanence of Paper for Printed Library Materials,
ANSI Z39.48—1984

Dedication

For my family Carla and Caralie, and especially for my
mother Faye and in memory of my father Carl Chrisco.

Table of Contents

LIST OF TABLES
ACKNOWLEDGEMENTS
INTRODUCTION
  Rationale
Chapter I. WAR COVERAGE   1
  Research on Perceptions   1
  Research on Editorials and War   2
Chapter II. METHOD   13
  Sample of Analysis   13
  Selected Newspapers   13
  Analysis   14
Chapter III. ANALYSIS of ACTORS and THEMES   17
  The *Jordan Times* (Jordan)   17
  The *Syria Times* (Syria)   27
  The *Arab News* (Saudi Arabia)   31
  The *United Arab Emirate News* (United Arab Emirates)   38
  The *Jerusalem Post* (Israel)   44
  The *Kayhan International* (Iran)   51
  Summary of Major Actors and Themes   59
Chapter IV. VALUES in the MIDDLE EAST PRESS   71
  The *Jordan Times* (Jordan)   71
  The *Syria Times* (Syria)   77
  The *Arab News* (Saudi Arabia)   82
  The *United Arab Emirate News* (United Arab Emirates)   89
  The *Jerusalem Post* (Israel)   94
  The *Kayhan International* (Iran)   100

Summary of Values   108
Chapter V. CONCLUSION   117
    Summary of Procedures   117
    Conclusions   117
    Discussion   119
    Recommendations for Further Studies   121
BIBLIOGRAPHY   123
INDEX   125

List of Tables

3.1. The role actors play in editorials in six
Middle Eastern newspapers   60

3.2. Macro and micro themes in editorials in
the *Jordan Times* and the *Syria Times* during
the Persian Gulf crisis and War   63

3.3. Macro and micro themes in editorials in the
Arab News and the *Emirate News* during the
Persian Gulf crisis and War   65

3.4. Macro and micro themes in editorials in the
Kayhan International and the *Jerusalem Post*
during the Persian Gulf crisis and War   67

Acknowledgments

I would like to thank Dr. Mazharul Haque for taking such an important part in helping me with the project. He is a true scholar who has contributed to every aspect of this work. Without his expert guidance and encouragement this work would not have been possible.

I would also like to thank Dr. Gene Wiggins, Dr. James Flanagan, and Dr. Art Kaul for giving me support and direction throughout this process.

Introduction

On August 2, 1990 Iraq's army invaded Kuwait. This invasion began a five-month standoff between the Iraqi army and the United Nations sanctioned allied forces culminating in a six-week long war beginning January 12, 1991 and ending February 28, 1991. The United States was a primary actor in the action. Unprecedented 24-hour coverage by the three major networks in the United States along with Cable News Network's domestic and worldwide coverage quickly turned the Persian Gulf War into the media event of the century.

Newspapers play an important part in informing and shaping public opinion. The newspaper reportage, its structure, production and restriction, helps set the agenda of the public, thereby contributing to a point of view from which the reader draws conclusions. These conclusions constitute perspectives from which war is justified with the reader ultimately backing or disavowing the actions of political leaders. The "just war" concept becomes not only of vital importance to the wagers of war, but, to the citizens who support the war.

This study deals with reactions and postures of the conflict zone newspapers during two separate periods of the Persian Gulf crisis and war. Pre-war and war editorials are examined in an effort to better understand the perceptions of various issues as they are presented and explained in the press of these nations. An examination of the consistency and a possible pattern of these editorials and commentaries during such clearly defined periods will lead to an understanding of the role of the press in what Lasswell calls the correlation function of the media (Lasswell, 1948).

The study of the editorials in the conflict zone provides a vehicle to examine and better understand issues that are important from a regional yet multinational and pluralistic perspective. An analysis of the editorials, provided a view of the perceptions various nations hold with regard to the United States, Iraq, and various other actors and issues surrounding the war. The study will give media scholars a better understanding of the various cultural perspectives from which a nation either justifies war or rejects it as a valid means of settling conflicts.

Following are some of the questions this study attempts to investigate: Who were the major participants during the pre-war and war period for each newspaper? What themes emerge concerning these actors? What values are denoted within the context of the various themes showing cultural and socioeconomic relationships within a nation? Are there values that apply to the whole region?

Chapter I
WAR COVERAGE

The creation of perceptions through the media has been the focus of media studies (Lippmann, 1922; Hyman and Sheatsley, 1947; Kuhn, 1970; Schudson, 1982). Media scholars have looked at perceptions in terms of our ability to structure and organize our world through information received through the mass media. This ability to tell the reader "what to think about" has been termed agenda setting. Even though agenda setting has been a concern of scholars for a long time, systematic studies began when McCombs and Shaw (1972) studied press agenda-setting during the 1968 presidential election campaign. Since then many studies and discussions have appeared in the literature. McCombs and Shaw (1972) found that undecided voters made decisions directly linked to the agenda set by the media. Funkhouser (1973) found through an extensive study of public opinion, press coverage, and statistical indicators representing reality throughout the 1960s, that, although public opinion and press coverage corresponded for the period, neither of the factors corresponded with statistical indicators. The media were creating their own reality and in doing so presented a world view that did not correspond to what was actually going on during the reportage of important issues such as the Viet Nam conflict and urban riots.

War reporting becomes a concern because it raises a different question of agenda setting in protecting the national interest by rallying the citizens at home. Similarly, editorials have long been considered an appropriate medium through which to study the press and its role during wartime. Lasswell (1935) spoke of our "symbolic environment" as being formed "by words, pictures, songs, slogans, parades, and similar devices" that "may be used to manipulate our collective attitudes"(p.146). He dubbed editors as one of the many growing number of symbol specialists who, although not directly considered propagandists, still "...may be very dependent upon propagandists for the symbols which they supply subscribers"(p.154).

Political warfare is linked with war coverage. Davison (1952) describes "Political Warfare" as:

> the use of communication to weaken the morale of enemy troops and encourage enemy troops and encourage surrenders, to weaken the morale of enemy civilians or to strengthen the morale of friendly troops and civilians (p. 18).

Editorials have been studied throughout the twentieth century as a mechanism to gain insight into the workings of international politics with revolutions and wars as a priority. Schillinger (1966) analyzed editorial comment at the time of the November 1917 Bolshevik Revolution. By investigating the British and U.S. newspaper coverage of the revolution she found that "Despite the ample forewarning and the acknowledged inevitability of its arrival, the actual Bolshevik takeover caught the newspaper world unprepared" (p. 11). News and editorials expressed an optimism and naivete, and political implications of a projected society under Bolshevism were ignored. Concern over Russia leaving World War I and an unrealistic perception of the Bolsheviks as "fanatic pacifists" who could not remain in power dominated editorials.

Schillinger (1966) concludes that the coverage lacked depth, accuracy, and objectivity. Reliable sources were difficult to locate, reporters with little knowledge about Russian history drew illogical conclusions. The revolutionaries were blamed for not issuing proper news releases and protecting journalists.

Brown (1937) examined news reports and editorials in nine U.S. papers for the pre-World-War period of 1912-1914. This examination produced the conclusion that the press did not explain events that would contribute to a better understanding of what was actually taking place in Europe.

News values determined the events that would be played up and the ones that would be ignored. America's interests were in local and domestic events. Brown concludes that the nine newspapers inadequately reported and interpreted events leading to World War I but did so because of the indifference of the American public to foreign affairs. Nationalism was blamed for this indifference, not the nationalism that Europe was experiencing with its "militant, aggressive, and selfishly concerned" press, but an insular nationalism.

World War II and the recognition of the power of the media created a need for scholars to examine and explain the duties of the press from a different perspective. Wartime censorship was the focal point for MacDougall(1942) as he believed that newspapers were responsible for teaching the reader how to read wartime news.

MacDougall (1942) states "This obligation exists because the irrational but very real fear that a large number of American newspaper readers have had during the past two and a half years of war propaganda now is being transferred to wartime censorship" (p.41). In addressing this fear of censorship by the American public, MacDougall explains four "lessons" that may aid the reader:

First, that any delays in news transmission or suppression will be in the interest of national safety....Something terrible has not happened with the establishment of the Office of Censorship.

Second, that censorship in a democracy, even in wartime, is entirely different from censorship in a totalitarian nation....Holding up or suppressing military secrets does not mean that the Bill of Rights has been suspended or that our democracy has been abandoned in favor of fascism.

Third, that news from battlefronts will be as complete and accurate in the future as it has been up to this time....American newspapers are to be congratulated for keeping their heads while radio was losing its.

Fourth, that censorship will not prevent comment and criticism....We must assure our readers particularly that our columnist seers will continue to do business as usual....

MacDougall put the reader's mind to rest on the issue of propaganda when he disavowed the need for it, and said, "Last time(WWI) we had to build up Kaiser Wilhelm as the embodiment of all the devilry on the other side of no man's land: we already have our devils—Hitler and now the Japanese"(p.45). This article not only gives a glimpse into the attitude of journalists during World War II and their way of explaining military censorship and adapting to it. In addition, the article introduces the threat of radio, a nonprint medium, because of a tendency to broadcast information too quickly thereby creating a threat to national security.

Canham(1942) delivered a critique of wartime reportage in connection with newspapers' obligation to get the facts. Sources were seen as the primary problem in restricting information. Access to sources by news agencies promoted a call to the U.S. press not to "take this lying down" (p.316). Playing down casualties was described as a propaganda technique as Canham said, "I was extremely interested to learn that the decision to hold back and play down American casualties, subsequently altered, was not an army or navy decision but a political or propagandist decision" (p.316).

This issue illustrates the quandary of formulating perceptions pertaining to both sides in a war. The sides defined are the military and the press, "...while the military man properly must press on the side of suppression, the newspaper man properly must press on the side of the public's need to know" (p.315).

Dewey(1967) provides an assessment of American attitudes toward the Soviet Union during the opening years of World War II through studying "shifts and turns" along with inaccurate assessments of events in editorials of the *New York Times*. Inconsistencies in alternately despising the Soviet Union, and embracing it as a friend, are reflected in editorials of the American papers that lack historical insight. The editors were also unable to wait to comment until significant trends became apparent. Dewey studies the *New York Times* as the most internationally-minded newspaper in the country which historically created, as well as reflected, public opinion.

Dewey begins his analysis with the August, 1939 editorial that "cheered the apparent end to the 'haggling and quibbling' over the pact which the Soviet Union was expected to make with France and Great Britain" (p.63). Later in the same month, after news of the Russo-German Non-Aggression Act of August 23, a *Times* editorial chose to approach the subject with optimism speculating that the pact and its disturbances, "might even lead to the realignment of Europe"(p.64).

Dewey then points to a number of inconsistencies in the editorial positions taken on Russia by the *New York Times*.

Viet Nam presented a unique challenge to the press. Emery (1971) describes the Viet Nam conflict as "the most thoroughly covered war in history" (p. 619). Extended and escalated American involvement in the war provided more than a decade of news coverage. Emery describes the "Quagmire" in which the media progressively found themselves. The State Department issued "press guidance" in 1962 forbidding "thoughtless" criticism of the Diem government. Press criticism was labelled uncooperative if they issued facts that pointed in a direction not consistent with U.S. policy.

Beginning in 1964, "the Five O'Clock Follies," a military briefing of the previous day's activities, was established. The briefings played an important part in the reporting of the war. Many reporters did not attend these meetings, and, if they did, they realized that information was being withheld or distorted through reports of inaccurate body counts and "precision bombing." Emery(1971) criticizes the press, despite its misgivings, for reporting these accounts as fact thereby creating "an illusion of conventional battle warfare when none really existed except in calculated situations" (p. 622).

According to Emery(1971), two reporters, Morley Safer of CBS in 1965, and Harrison Salisbury of the *New York Times* in 1966, were instrumental in changing perceptions on the part of U.S. citizens at home. Safer exposed marine procedure in "The Burning of the Village of Cam Ne," while Salisbury filed reports from inside North Vietnam telling and showing through photographs indiscriminate and inefficient bombing by U.S. flyers.

Public reaction was mixed. The *New York Times* was angrily attacked for running Salisbury's story, while Safer's film was considered "too realistic." For some segments of the American public the press lacked in credibility, while for others, the credibility of the Pentagon suffered.

By 1971, following the Tet offensive of 1968, the decision of President Johnson's withdrawal from the 1968 presidential race, and Richard Nixon's institution of "Vietnamization" policy in 1969, news reports from Viet Nam came closer to representing the reality of what was going on in that country. While censorship by the U.S. military command in Saigon had remained minimal for the press throughout the war, the press had to contend with the South Vietnamese government and political critics at home(Emery, 1971).

Susan Welch's (1972) study of the American press and Indochina for the years 1950-56, surveys a segment of the press during a series of related foreign policy decisions made by the United States. The study concentrated on newspapers including *New York Times*, the *Chicago Tribune*, the *Washington Post*, and the *San Francisco Chronicle*. These newspapers were examined for the frequency of articles, editorials, and signed columns dealing with the role, or the potential role, of the United States' involvement in Indochina. Locations within the papers, the tone and content of each item, and whether the news story was used as a background story, a signed column, or an editorial was noted. More specifically, the study examines:

> 1. the quality and content of the press coverage of the American role in Indochina, 2. how and why the press defined the situation as it did, and, 3. some possible implications of the behavior of the press for rational foreign policy decision-making (p.207).

Editorial positions in the four newspapers were categorized into three broad sets consisting of those predominantly favorable to the position taken by the Administration, the pro-French government of Vietnam or the French themselves, those neutral toward the United States or Allied policy in Indochina, and, finally, those predominantly opposed to policies being pursued in Indochina by the United States and its Allies, if these allied actions were being taken with the approval of the United States (Welch, 1972).

The following table indicates Editorial Support of Administration Positions during Selected Periods:

	New York Times	Washington Post	San Francisco Chronicle	Chicago Tribune
Favorable	43.7%	35.3%	50.0%	12.5%
Neutral	46.9%	53.1%	33.3%	12.5%
Unfavorable	9.4%	11.6%	16.7%	75.0%
Support Ratio*	4.7	3.0	3.0	17.0

*Support Ratio=number of positive editorials divided by the number of negative editorials (p.213).

Welch concludes that as early as 1954 three assumptions, helped by the press, had been fixed with the public. First, Indochina was an area of vital interest to United States. Secondly, Indochina was being challenged by a clear case of Communist aggression that had to be stopped in the U.S. interest. Finally, if the Indochinese knew all the facts, they would naturally support the United States in any action to stop the aggression. Editorials never challenged these assumptions.

Questions from the newspapers concerned issues of incremental actions, such as should aid or troops be sent? Should the United States tell France what to do? Should the United States set up a formal Asian alliance or should the matter be handled by the United Nations? Most sources involved decision-makers in the U.S. Administration consequently reinforcing news stories and editorials toward its point of view.

Welch concludes with the assertion that although the press cannot be held to have sole responsibility for "...either Administration policy in Indochina or the relatively recent rise of dissent toward that policy," it did play a crucial role in sustaining the perceptions of the mass and elite public by the basic assumptions it acted upon. These assumptions, as represented in news reporting and backed up by discussion in the editorials, were the Administration's view of the Indochina situation.

Shipman (1983) cited a number of editorials in the *Wall Street Journal*, in which the daily accused the *New York Times*, and "the media" in general of "romanticizing" Salvadoran revolutionaries. President Reagan attacked the media for "downbeat reporting" on El Salvador prompting quick reaction on the part of the media with editorial responses denouncing the President's attack.

Editorials and their power to create perceptions are illustrated in this study. President Reagan made public complaints of the media's reportage of U.S. policy in El Salvador. Major newspapers responded editorially to the President's attacks, and *Times'* Executive Editor A.M. Rosenthal flew to El Salvador to assure unbiased reporting.

In his analysis Shipman employs Hayakawa's trichotomy - report sentences, inference sentences, and judgement sentences. He used this trichotomy to measure objectivity in the writing of news stories in the *New York Times* concerning the war in El Salvador. He also wanted to determine if the number of influence and judgement sentences decreased in the *Times* after the *Journal* attacks.

The researcher was also interested in determining if the editorial attacks by the *Journal* had any effect on the *Times'* reporting. This would be shown by an increase in the number of attributed sentences that took place after the attack.

Results indicated that the *Times'* reportage did not change as a result of the *Journal's* attack. The low number of judgement sentences seemed to indicate that "*Times* writers and editors exercised care not to put opinion in the form of judgements into news stories" (p.721). The number of attributed sentences in the *Times* did not increase, but, decreased significantly after the *Journal's* attack.

While this study shows that editorial attack was not answered by the *New York Times* which seemed to keep opinion out of its reporting (judgement sentences are considered the least objective) and did not respond in its editorials by attributing more reports to sources (a sign of increased objectivity), the findings do not present an adequate measure of objectivity in the news. Equally important, however, is what is not reported. A study designed to measure bias with the methodology used by Shipman could not possibly do an adequate job of measuring bias by omission.

Alan Jay Zaremba (1988) examines mass communication and international politics from the perspective of press reactions to the 1973 Arab-Israeli War. This case study looks at six newspapers from countries throughout the world in order to understand the perceptions of the public by analyzing editorials in these newspapers under the premise that "newspapers...inform and shape public opinion" (p.1). By gauging reports and consistency of specific events within editorials, not only subjective attitudes regarding who was right or wrong, but also, information describing actual events can be juxtaposed.

The six newspapers chosen: the *Daily Graphic of Ghana*, the *Times of London of Great Britain*, the *Asahi Evening News of Japan*, the *Straits Times of Singapore*, the *Moscow News of the U.S.S.R.*, and the *New York Times of the United States*, represented North America, Europe, Asia, Africa, Southeast Asia, and the Far East. English language newspapers written either for or by nationals were chosen.

The researcher used content analysis as an objective and systematic method for analyzing and quantifying media content. The following categories were tabulated according to the number of times they appeared in reference to either Arabs or Israelis:

aggression
land legitimacy
imperialism

intransigence
terrorism
peace seeking
culpability
action justification
Zionism issue
super power culpability
oil diplomacy (p.7-8)

Perceptual divergences on key issues became apparent from examination of the results. Arabs were considered the aggressors by the *New York Times, Straits Times, Asahi Evening News,* and *London Times* while the Israelis were seen as the aggressor by the *Moscow News* and the *Daily Graphic.* On other categories, the newspapers proved divided as well, for example *Moscow News, Daily Graphic, Asahi Evening News,* and *Times of London* saw the Israelis as imperialistic while the *Straits Times* and *New York Times* described neither as imperialistic. In the peace seeking category, the newspapers' perceptions were also divergent.

Zaremba's research stresses the perceptions of specific events and issues during a war. These perceptions become important when public opinion comes into play in any war. Public support for war is important to political leaders who are waging a war, or defending a nation's policy. These perceptions are not only important to the countries immediately involved, but to other nations as well. In showing the differences in perspectives held on such issues by the newspapers, Zaremba has taken media research away from a national perspective and placed the media's role within an international spectrum.

Pre-war and Persian Gulf War coverage by the press became an immediate issue both during and after the War. A Gannett Foundation Report (1991) provides a quantitative and qualitative analysis of the war coverage that addresses the role of the press during wartime. The study analyzed "...not only the news media's coverage of the gulf war but the many issues surrounding that coverage" (p. xi). A range of methods were used to examine various topics namely, historical analysis, surveys of journalists, media executives and technology experts, a bibliometric search of databases for language, a quantitative look at the air time and space, a content analysis of editorial pages, a roundtable discussion of the media's performance, an assessment of public opinion, and a survey analysis of polls conducted during the war.

Findings pertaining to issues of war coverage were as follows:

1. Tracing the history of censorship from the Civil War through the Persian Gulf War, they found that although censorship was not directly practiced in the Gulf War, severe restrictions were placed on press access to the war zone restricting the availability and flow of information. This practice, which was perfected during the Grenada invasion, was in sharp contrast to access in covering the Viet Nam War. The military, as admitted by it, "...used the press to promulgate its own policies as well as to spread disinformation to the Iraqis" (p. xii). And finally, several lawsuits separately challenged these restrictions "to no avail" signifying that similar kinds of restrictions will be enforced during future actions.

2. Correspondents surveyed brought to light that the pool system had many problems. Although it worked well for the military it, did not serve the specific needs of the media (p. xii). There were too few pools, with frequent lack of cooperation and infighting among press members. Lack of access to people and places rather than direct censorship, hindered correspondents in gathering "real news."

3. Technology made the first "real-time" war possible. The media incurred heavy costs in providing the technology to provide coverage that included key technologies such as electronic mail and computer-to-computer communications, and satellite transmission.

4. News coverage of the war dominated news broadcasts and front pages causing other issues such as the recession to "fade" onto the background. Editorials, while providing "thoughtful responses to key policy decisions made by the Bush administration" primarily reflected the government's viewpoint and "expressed little dissent'(p.xii).

5. Public opinion polls showed that Americans generally perceived the media as doing a good job. They approved of the restrictions imposed on the press by the military. Television was used as America's "preeminent source of information" with CNN(61%) ranking first followed by ABC(12%) and NBC(7%) and CBS(7%) trailing behind.

Under the title "The Goals of War:Newspaper Editorial coverage at Defining Moments of the Crisis" researchers surveyed unsigned editorials in five influential United States newspapers. The report reached one overall conclusion:

> In fact, at virtually every stage of the conflict, these papers' editorials refused to wander beyond the parameters of the discussion as it unfolded in Washington; while they differed in tone and degree, they displayed con-

siderable consensus in their views of the Middle East, its people, and the interests of the United States in the region(p.53).

While "thoughtfully" responding to key policy decisions made by the president the only dissent was usually over "tactics and timing rather than goals and principles" (p. 63). Saddam Hussein remained the "quintessential bad guy" creating a perception of reality that pervaded the crisis.

Technology provided instant coverage of the war while the military supplied and controlled access to information transmitted through technology. And, finally, a limited perspective was presented to the public by the media under the guise of editorial discussion. This perspective not only depended upon the restricted access to information by reporters but exposed the press' hesitancy to bring up questions that may challenge government policy.

Because of the nature of wartime reportage this stance is not only typical during wars, but, is also apparent in critical policy forming stages that preceded the war. Conclusions can, therefore, be drawn that the media aid significantly in the acceptance of policy, not just during, but, before a war. The reality and perceptions of the media consumer are also limited to views proposed by the government and backed-up by the media.

A number of studies have been conducted by scholars examining the reportorial or editorial coverage of different wars by the U.S. press. This study by examining the editorials of newspapers from six countries in the conflict zone, which had different degrees of involvement in the Persian Gulf War of 1990-91, attempts to provide important perspectives on the war, and hense, fills a significant void in the war coverage literature.

Chapter II
METHOD

Sample for Analysis

Newspaper editorials were used for the study representing opinions of the newspapers. Signed commentaries, post-editorials and op-ed pieces were not used. The editorials for this study appeared in six newspapers over a seven-month period beginning August 2, 1990 when Iraq invaded Kuwait and ending February 28, 1991 when the war ended. Two time periods were studied, the pre-war period, August 2, 1990 through January 11, 1991, and the war period, January 12, 1991 through February 28, 1991. Approximately 600 editorials were indentified.

Selected Newspapers

The newspapers that provide the editorials have been selected on the basis of papers representing the region of conflict. Each newspaper selected is an English language newspaper. Availability and publishing affiliation with a major national language newspaper determined the choice of newspapers.

The following is a list of newspapers representing the conflict zone:

Arab News (Saudi Arabia). The *Arab News* is published in Jeddah by the Saudi Research and Marketing Company. It has a circulation of 110,000.

Emirates News (United Arab Emirates). The *Emirates News* is published in Abu Dhabi by Al-Ittihad Press and Publishing Corporation. It has a circulation of 15,000.

Jerusalem Post (Israel). The *Jerusalem Post* is published in Jerusalem. It is an independent newspaper with a circulation of 60,000.

Jordan Times (Jordan). The *Jordan Times* is published in Amman by the Jordan Press Establishment. It has a circulation of 15,000. The Jordan Press Establishment also publishes the *Ar-Rai*, an independent daily, in Arabic, with a circulation of 80,000.

Kayhan International (Iran). The *Kayhan International* is published in Teheran and is part of the *Kayhan Universal* which is published in Farsi. The combined circulation of the two is 350,000.

Syria Times (Syria). The *Syria Times* is published in Damascus by the Tishrin Foundation for Press and Publication and has a circulation of 12,000. The Tishrin Foundation for Press and Publication also publishes the *Tishrin*, in Arabic, with a circulation of 70,000.

Analysis

Major participants or actors within each editorial were listed and analyzed over the pre-war and war periods. The frequency of references to actors and their contribution to the solution of the conflict or hindering the solution were also noted. In this analysis, metaphors and other descriptive devices were noted to illustrate the role each actor is assigned in the editorial.

Thematic Structures were examined with the purpose of discovering themes and subthemes discussed within the editorials. Teun A. van Dijk (1988) provides a systematic analysis in which textual structures are examined to explicate themes or topics. This process involves the semantic theory by which paragraphs within the editorial are examined to establish the macrostructures (the larger stretches of talk or text). According to van Dijk, "Topics are crucial in the overall understanding of the text, e.g., in the establishment of global coherence; and they act as semantic, top-down control on local understanding at the microlevel" (p.35).

Subthemes were analyzed and the microthemes were compared across the specific time periods to show what role they play in supporting the macrothemes.

It is assumed that editorials are written to explain and comment upon issues concerning the national interests of countries represented by each newspaper. Acting upon this assumption within the cultural perspective of the reader, we can also assume that arguments within the editorial comment will be directed to the reader within their cultural definitions of what are acceptable strategies concerning conflict.

And finally, values were noted from the editorial arguments presented. This analysis is based upon axiological precepts (Lasswell 1948, 1960; Frondizi,1963; & Brennan and Hahn, 1990). Acting upon these precepts, that values denote an essence toward an object, values are categorized according to the verbs, adverbs, and adjectives used in the editorial to denote the actors' perceived role in conflict resolution.

Further, Rokeach (1968) defines values as "an enduring belief that a specific mode of conduct or end-state of existence is personally or socially preferable to alternate modes of conduct or end-state existence" (160). Sillars (1991) defines value statements as expressing, "a judgement about what is the preferred end state or means of action" (129). Values, when viewed as human concepts embodied in signs, therefore, define the culture implied by the text.

Consequently, values in texts can be explicit but are more likely to be implicit. Gans (1980) says that values are found, "between the lines—in what actors and activities are reported or ignored, and in how they are described" (40). By "reading between the lines", values are determined by noting undesirable actions of actors along with descriptive negative connotations. If these actions are considered undesirable, then they implicitly are referenced against values that are desirable. It also becomes necessary to note values that are taken-for-granted and, therefore, not mentioned. By assuming that the reader will understand and process commentary based on basic systems of shared values that are not explicit in the editorials, we can presume these "taken-for-granteds" as values.

Finally, values were grouped in what Gans (1980) calls, "value clusters." Value clusters separate topical values, manifested in explicit statements, into enduring implicit values found over a period of time (41). A value hierarchy was established for each newspaper over the defined time periods.

These hierarchical value clusters were compared within the conflict zone from the perspective of press representation. This analysis shows similarities and differences in the editorials based on the national and cultural perspectives of each nation.

Chapter III
ANALYSIS of ACTORS and THEMES

Analysis of editorials appearing in the six Middle East newspapers indicates a variety of participants or actors and themes. A diversity of perspectives concerning who was the aggressor, the peacemaker, the responsible party, the victim, and the defender, clearly illustrates differences among Middle East newspapers during the Persian Gulf crisis and war. These differences are explained through an examination of expectations based on various institutions, organizations, leaders, allies, and enemies from, not only the present, but, from the past, both recent and not so recent.

Major actors and themes emerged from the expectations, predictions, speculations, and recommendations in the editorial. Actors and themes from each newspaper are reported separately. A concluding section to this chapter compares actors and themes from the perspectives of the six nations.

The Jordan Times

Forty-three editorials were available for the seven- month period, from August, 1990 through February, 1991 for analysis. Within these forty-three editorials thirty-nine dealt with the Persian Gulf crisis and war.

The Arab Nation quickly became the primary actor with Arab unity and solidarity as the underlying, pervasive theme throughout the pre-war and war period. Early in the editorials, the *Jordan Times* introduced the Arab-unity theme which ran throughout the period("Early reaction, more to come," August 3, 1990). Other themes surfaced and receded concerning Arab solidarity or its division. A discussion of the Arab-unity theme requires an analysis of the macro and micro themes recurring within the text. These included, Arabs-as-peacemakers, King Hussein(Jordan)-as-a-peacemaker (in favor of dialogue), Saddam Hussein-as-the-strong-Arab, Saddam Hussein(Iraq)-as-the-peacemaker, Jordan-as-a-victim, Arab Nation-divided, United States-drives-wedge, U.S.-equals-Israel, linkage (an attempt to "link" Saddam's invasion to the Israeli/Palestinian issue), double-standard, U.S.-as-aggressor, Saudi Arabia-as-a-victim, foreign-troops-on-Arab-soil, U.S.-oil-conspiracy, Bush's personal crusade, allies-support-aggression, and, UN responsibility. These themes were supported in an interlacing of arguments discussing the history of how the United States became the aggressor in the region and other countries became victims. Through the use of actors and the roles they have played in reference to the proposed aggressors and victims, other, less mentioned, but equally important, micro themes emerged. Some of these micro themes are, Saddam-defends-Arabs-against-Israel, Saddam-gestures-to-Iran, and Israel-benefits.

Arab Unity Theme

Analysis revealed that the Arab unity theme is an important macro theme throughout the time period. A number of micro themes, the Arabs-as-peacemakers, Saddam-as-a-strong-Arab, U.S.-drives-a-wedge, linkage, and King Hussein(Jordan)-as-peacemaker, contributed to the development of the Arab unity theme.

From the beginning of the crisis, the Arab-unity theme, with a call for an Arab solution, is apparent in the *Jordan Times'* approach to the problem of Iraq invading Kuwait. Consequently, Iraq's invasion is seen as an inter-Arab problem with its solution the responsibility of the Arab Nation. In the editorial, "Early reaction, more to come," appearing on August 3, 1990, the day after Iraq invaded Kuwait, Saddam Hussein is described as a strong Arab who is countering the "Zionist" threat. Saddam is seen as a symbol of steadfastness and a challenge to Israel which wishes to redraw the map of the Middle East, while Saddam's annexation of Kuwait is seen as an attempt to redraw the map within pan-Arab interests. The *Times* reminds the readers of Jordan's oil dependency on Iraq coupled with the expected aid money, from Iraq. In the following day's editorial, "Feverish campaigns and hidden facts," August 4, 1990, a recent history of Iraq's problems with Kuwait is delineated. President Hussein addresses Arab leaders in a letter dated July 14 explaining Iraq's trouble with Kuwait for not paying its war debt(Iran-Iraq war). This problem came at a time when the United States' propaganda campaign against Iraq had reached "a feverish pitch" concerning Saddam's chemical weapons development. At the same time, however, Kuwait reneged on its war debt thereby forcing Iraq to use its oil earnings to finance military advances. In this early editorial, the *Times* proposed a linkage, the idea that Saddam Hussein invaded Kuwait in order to further the Palestinian cause in Israel. In the editorial, Iraq is seen as defending the Arab Nation, whose predominant focus is the Israeli/Palestinian territorial issue. The United States at the same time, is equated with Israel because of its support of, not only chemical, but, nuclear weapons for Israel. Hence, the double-standard theme also begins in the first few days of the period and is referred to throughout the crisis and war. On August 5, 1990 this theme is reinforced in relation to Israel and the United States when the *Jordan Times* says that the United States has put its interests (oil) ahead of Arab rights by trying to impose cheaper oil prices on the world. In addition, the United States is considered "arrogant" as it "drives a wedge" in Arab unity by supporting Russian Jews resettling in the disputed territories, a decision harmful to the Palestinians, and, therefore, to the Arab Nation.

Establishing Iraq's invasion of Kuwait as an inter-Arab problem that should be solved within the Arab nation and thus the Arab League, King Hussein emerged early in the discussion as the peacemaker who looked upon intervention from the West, and especially from the United States, as an escalation of tensions rather than a solution. On August 6, 1990, the *Times* refers to King Hussein's call for an Arab answer rather than a foreign interventionist one ("Interventionist policies would not work"). It also suggests that two options proposed by the United States, the economic boycott and the use of military force, are both bad. The first, because a boycott would take time, thereby driving up the price of oil, and, in the event of use of military force, a war could reach a huge scale and give Iraq an opportunity to destroy many oil fields.

Arabs Divided

Analysis helped reveal a number of micro themes that contributed to the Arabs-divided theme. These themes began with King Hussein-as-the-peacemaker among the Arab nations and developed into the Jordan-as-the-victim of pan-Arab oil disputes and the U.S.-as-the-aggressor which by its interventionist policies was dividing the Arab Nation members. Throughout the editorials the problem of Iraq invading Kuwait remained an Arab problem that should be solved within an Arab solution.

Equally important within the King Hussein-as-peacemaker theme is the understanding of the underlying importance of oil as, not only a U.S. interest in the conflict, but, the reason for division within the Arab Nation. Arab diversity and Saddam Hussein's strength within that diversity is explained in a North versus South scenario ("Dream lives on," August 10, 1990). The Arab East is divided into the North which is oil-poor and the oil-rich South, with the United States (Israel's ally) associated with the South. The oil-rich South (most notably, Saudi Arabia) condescend to the West and squander its wealth while the North is mistreated. This division of oil wealth within the Arab Nation forces the poor Northern countries, of which Jordan is one, to side with the strength of Saddam Hussein in solving any oil disputes with the Southern Arabs.

The Jordan-as-a-victim theme was established early during the period. Beginning August 8, 1990 the issue of promised aid to Jordan from Kuwait ($135m) and Iraq ($50m) was discussed while early responses to the invasion by the international community included the freezing of Iraqi and Kuwaiti assets. Jordan's reliance on Iraqi petroleum, coupled with both countries' landlocked geographical position, except for Jordan's port of Aqaba on the Red Sea, further emphasize the issue of Jordan's economic dependence on Iraq as a major trading partner.

An equally important issue was the refugees entering Jordan from Kuwait. These refugees represented not only, Egyptians, Indians, and others, but, a large number of Jordanians who were contributing to Jordan's economy through their jobs in Kuwait.

The Jordan-as-victim theme developed as a result of the United Nations embargo on Iraq. On August 12, 1990, the *Times* declares that sanctions against Iraq are not in the interest of Jordan ("Sanctions in balance"). Even though Turkey had been compensated at the rate of

five million dollars a day by the United States using Arab oil money for
shutting down Iraqi pipelines and upholding sanctions, Jordan, had not
received any aid. Similarly, Jordan was threatened with closure of its
only port, Aqaba on the Red Sea, if it did not comply with the sanctions
against Iraq. The *Times* points out that Jordan had blockaded nonessen-
tial goods and was suffering for following this honorable course of action while other countries in the region were being compensated for
complying with the sanctions.

The *Times* editorializes about the U.S. interventionist policy victimizing Jordan (August 19, 1990 in "Early reactions more to come"). The
newspaper points out that the Jordanians, particularly the Palestinians in
Jordan, feel that Saddam Hussein is challenging the Zionist expansionist territorial and, therefore, they support Saddam Hussein. Accordingly, Jordan which, by this time, is experiencing grave economic
difficulties as a result of the sanctions against Iraq, is also being un-
justly punished by the United States. Iraq's invasion of Kuwait is
placed in the context of an Arab problem that should be solved by the
Arabs. Consequently, the *Times* calls Arabs to avoid haste and seek an
answer with the Arab nation's interests of development, democracy,
and modernization as its basis. Jordan's victimization is handled by the
Times through various appeals to the Arabs for Arab solidarity in solving an Arab problem in the context of an Arab solution. Accordingly,
by citing explicit examples of attacks on Jordan's economy, the United
States is labeled as the primary aggressor upon, not only Arabs in general, but, Jordan in particular. Thus, an editorial on September 23,
1990, calls for an end to the United States imposed boycott on Iraq and
compensation to Jordan for direct and indirect economic losses that resulted from Jordan honoring this unpopular U.N. resolution("Equitable
share"). And, on October 24, 1990, the *Times* mentions Jordan's threats
to take the matter of the United States "pirating" ships entering Jordan's
port of Aqaba to the United nations. The editorial says that Jordan is
being punished for excluding the West, and the United States in particular, in its call for an Arab solution ("Piracy must end").

After the United States Congress denied Jordan $50m in military aid
in October, the newspaper addressed the issue within the Jordan-as-victim and Arabs-as-peacemakers themes. President Bush is said to use a
"carrot and stick" approach whereby he and the U.S. Senate hold out
the proposal of writing off $50m worth of Jordan's military debt in ex-
change for Jordan changing its stand from a peaceful Arab solution to

an aggressive one. However, the House of Representatives disapproves of the debt forgiveness, thereby giving the *Times* the opportunity to say that Jordan's peace proposal and its support of Iraq cannot be bought (October 28, 1990 "Pressure won't work").

Later, the *Times* discusses Bettino Craxi, former prime minister of Italy and now a U.N. official, who, while acting as the U.N. secretary general's personal representative, has called for a moratorium and debt restructuring for countries which have lost money because of the sanctions imposed upon Iraq. The *Times* cries for help for Jordan and further explains its situation by claiming to be victimized because of its views concerning Iraq and Kuwait. Jordan-as-peacemaker theme is again presented when the *Times* claims that Jordan's demand for a peaceful solution is the primary reason for it to be singled out (October 29, 1990 "The word from Craxi").

Arabs-Divided (United States and Isreal)

The alliance between Israel and the United States provided micro themes that contributed to Arabs being divided over claims by Saddam Hussein that his invasion of Kuwait was linked with the Palestinian/Israeli territorial issue.　Saddam Hussein-as-a-strong-Arab theme emerged as the United States was accused of using a double-standard in dealing with Israel.　The Israel-benefits, the linkage, and the U.S.-equals-Israel themes each contributed to the discussion by the *Times* of the Israeli/Palestinian issue as a legitimate Arab problem.

Underlying the Arabs-divided theme is the Western-double-standard theme. Through this theme the United States' actions and reactions are compared to Israel's in the Palestinian territories (UN resolution 673), and Iraq's occupation of Kuwait (UN resolutions 660). While the double-standard theme is used throughout the span of the crisis and war to validate the U.S. as aggressor, it also supported many other micro themes. Accordingly, Israel-benefits theme, the linkage (Israeli-Palestinian issue) theme, and the U.S.-equals-Israel themes are developed with subtle uses of each theme working together, both explicitly and implicitly.

Specifically, on October 27, 1990 in "Racism or hypocrisy," Washington is said to send aid to Israel which does not abide by the U.N. resolutions, while Iraq, a strong Arab nation, is being forced by Washington to abide by the U.N. resolutions to withdraw from Kuwait. The United States is, therefore, declared racist and anti-Arab, while, Iraq and Jordan (implied) work specifically for solutions within an Arab framework.

Israel and the Palestinian problem, along with Israel benefiting from the distraction caused by Iraq's invasion of Kuwait of both the Arab Nation and the international community recur as micro themes throughout the period. An important point in the Israel-benefits theme occurs in October when Israeli police killed 17 Palestinians at the Temple Mount in Jerusalem. The *Times* points to Israel's part in the Temple Mount killings, followed by its refusal to allow a U.N. investigating committee into Israel, and challenges the International community to enforce U.N. resolutions concerning Israel. Arabs are, therefore, seen as victims with Saddam Hussein as the strong Arab who is trying to expose the Israelis for what they are, the primary threat against Arab solidarity(on October, 21, 1990, "Eyes on the U.N. again," and again on November 27, 1990, "Natural linkage").

Saddam Hussein(Iraq)-as-Peacemaker

Analysis revealed that Saddam Hussein emerged as a peacemaker in the editorials. Several micro themes contributed to this progression, namely, the Saddam-gestures-to-Iran, Saddam-as-strong-Arab, the U.S.-as-aggressor, Bush's-personal crusade, and, the Saudi Arabia-as-a-victim.

At the same time, and equally important, is Iraq's role as a peacemaker with Saddam Hussein as the principal actor. Throughout the crisis President Saddam Hussein is shown as a strong Arab who works within the Arab Nation to solve problems that are strictly Arab. Kuwait is seen as a wayward Arab brother who, after accepting Saddam's protection during the Iran-Iraq war, reneged on debts owed for that protection, while, Saddam defends Arab solidarity in its ongoing Israeli-Palestinian problem.

During the prewar period Saddam's peacemaking efforts through its gestures to Iran were hailed as bold and positive. In August, the *Times* points out that Saddam is attempting to solve disputes with Iran concerning borders, territory, water, and POWs that have arisen out of the Iran-Iraq War. These attempts are seen by the newspaper as positive moves to resolve the Arab-Persian conflict without foreign intervention while the United States discredits them as only tactical ones (August 16, 1990, "Iraq move versus Iran:Bold and positive").

On August 20, 1990, the *Times* again praised Iraq for a gesture toward a resolution to the crisis ("Kuwait:A free zone?"). The Iraqi government proposed to solve the monetary problems caused by the freezing of Iraqi and Kuwaiti assets and international sanctions, by making Kuwait a free zone. This move is seen as positive by the *Jordan Times* because it would open Kuwaiti banks that could not immediately adapt to banking laws of Iraq. Although observers remained skeptical, the offer by Iraq is seen by the *Times* as a serious proposal to solve the problems imposed upon the Arabs as a result of Iraq's invasion of Kuwait.

Saddam's offer of oil to the third world was also seen as having strong pan-Arab dimensions when the *Jordan Times* discussed the offer within the North-South Arab framework (September 12, 1990 stunt or blunt step?"). The oil-rich Arabs in the south consider the offer thoughtful and timely because of the global implications of inflated oil prices. This economic and political solution would allow the South to minimize exporting the crisis to developing countries through inflated oil prices. Saddam's offer is seen as a way to prevent a further division between the haves and have-nots by providing the North with cheap oil and, therefore, eliminating oil as a factor in Arab loyalties. Saudi Arabia and other rich Arab countries could continue to sell oil at inflated prices to the industrial West which has the ability to pay. Hence, Saddam's offer is seen as a chance to ally the Arab Nation with Iraq, and force the United States to explain its decision to dismiss the offer as propaganda.

Any offers by Saddam to withdraw from Kuwait, but with concessions, placed Saddam in the peacemaker role. While President Bush's reaction to Saddam Hussein's offer to withdraw from Kuwait except for disputed oil fields and port, is presented as an irrational one. The newspaper focuses on Bush demonizing Saddam Hussein through his comparisons of Saddam to Nazi war criminals when a peaceful solution to the problem is needed. And, Bush's reaction in which he accuses Iraqi soldiers of taking Kuwaiti babies from incubators and killing Kuwaiti boys for distributing leaflets is countered by the *Jordan Times* which considers Saddam's offer reasonable and thus capable of solving the problem in the framework of a peaceful Arab solution (on October 18, 1990, in the editorial "Talk peace not war").

Other offers by Saddam to withdraw from Kuwait, including the actual withdrawal on February 26, 1991, portray Saddam as the cornered

Arab who is doing all he can toward a peaceful resolution of the war. On February 23, 1991, in the editorial "No capitulation," President Bush is again said to be unreasonable as he misinterprets Baghdad's formal acceptance of an eight-point peace plan that has been worked out with "sober" members (the Soviet Union) of the international community. This editorial absolves Saddam Hussein of responsibility for the war and justifies Iraq's resolve to resist the ground war that is now inevitable. On February 26, 1991, the *Times* describes Iraq's forced withdrawal from Kuwait as Saddam's last attempt to save lives and avert destruction ("Step closer to peace"). With Iraq emerging in the end as the peacemaker, the *Times* says that the West must take advantage of Iraq's decision and work toward that peace.

The U.S.-as-aggressor is a macro theme running throughout the period. Micro themes supporting the U.S.-as-aggressor are, the foreign troops on Arab soil, U.S.-oil-conspiracy, Bush's-personal-crusade, the U.S.- equals-Israel, the allies-behind-aggression (U.S. and Britain), and the U.N.-responsibility.

While early editorials linked the United States with Israel thereby reinforcing the West's assault on Arab solidarity and an Arab solution, the United States was, at the same time, mentioned as an interventionist nation which brought foreign troops to Arab soil in order to protect its own interests by controlling Middle East oil. Through the micro theme, foreign troops on Arab soil, Saudi Arabia is shown as a victim of U.S. intervention when it allows foreign (mainly U.S.) troops to base and build within its boundaries. President Bush is said to "beat the war drums" and, in doing so, convince Saudi Arabia that U.S. troops are needed to defend it from an imminent Iraqi attack (August 7, 1990 "Tips of interest to U.S. policy-makers,"). This micro theme is reinforced throughout the period with reference to Gorbachev justifying the troops in Saudi Arabia as defensive and temporary (on September 16, 1990), while the *Times*, later in the time period, challenges Saudi Arabia to be daring and bold to overcome the interventionist policy of the United States (November 22, 23, 1990 titled "Democracy wins").

Bush's personal crusade also emerges as a micro theme during the period. While supporting the macro theme, the U.S.-as-the-aggressor, the Bush's-personal-crusade theme squares off President Bush, the interventionist, against Saddam Hussein, the good Arab. The Bush's-personal-crusade theme, becomes more personal when Bush is described as "Beating the war drums," in an August 7, 1990 editorial. The *Times* further criticized Bush when his policy against Arabs was described as personal and emotional ("Medicine deadlier than disease," on August 22, 1990). This theme persists with Bush editorialized as maneuvering through "zig zag" courses with China, Paris and Moscow while trying to get the use of force sanctioned by the U.N. Security Council.

Conclusion

Analysis of the actors and themes throughout the seven-month period, August, 1990 through February, 1991 reveal the Arab Nation, Iraq and Saddam Hussein, Jordan and King Hussein, the international community and the United States, and Israel as primary actors. Yet it is equally clear, however, that each of these actors falls within a general and overlapping macro theme of Arab solidarity. In addressing the problem of Iraq invading another Arab state, the United States quickly became the interventionist force whose only interest was to protect its oil interests along with the interests of its ally, Israel. Arabs-as-peacemakers theme developed through the calling of a number of summits where various Arab nations were placed within the context of either supporting Arab solidarity or causing a breach in the Arab solidarity.

From the beginning, the United States is portrayed as supporting Arab division in order to protect its primary oil interest in the Middle East. All alliances, both international and pan-Arab, were based upon oil and its control. At the same time, however, the Israeli-Palestinian issue, which is deeply rooted in the history of conflict within the Arab League, was linked to the Gulf crisis and war. The United States, as the aggressor, was quickly equated with Israel through historical references and the double-standard theme.

Iraq and Saddam Hussein-as-peacemaker theme also emerged intertwined with the Arab solidarity and solution themes. Underlying this theme was the right of Arabs to solve Arab conflicts within a pan-Arab solution through dialogue. Saddam Hussein was seen as contributing to this dialogue through offers of withdrawal from Kuwait, while President Bush was seen as an emotionally-driven man who would stop at nothing short of Saddam's destruction.

Macro and Micro Themes

Arab-Unity
   Arabs-as-peacemakers

    King Hussein(Jordan)-as-peacemaker
    Linkage
    Saddam Hussein(Iraq)-as-peacemaker
    Saddam Hussein-as-strong-Arab
    Saddam-defends-Arabs-against-Israel
    Saddam-gestures-to-Iran
    U.N.-responsibility
Arabs-divided
    Jordan-as-victim
    Saudi Arabia-as-victim
    Israel-benefits
    U.S.-drives-wedge
    Double-standard
    Foreign troops-on-Arab-soil
    U.S.-as-aggressor
    U.S.-equals-Israel
    Allies-support-aggression
    U.S.-oil-conspiracy
    Bush's-personal-crusade

The Syria Times

Editorials in the *Syria Times* were available for the pre-war period only, from August, 1990, through December 1990. Over the five-month time period there were only sixteen editorials pertaining to the Persian Gulf crisis which were unsigned.

Two Macro themes, Arab-unity and Arabs-divided, dominated the editorials. Major actors consisted of national actors (Syria, Iraq, Israel, and the United States) and leaders of nations (President Al-Assad and President Bush), with the Arab Nation playing an important role in the narrative.

Arab-Unity and Arabs-Divided (Two Macro Themes)

The macro themes running through the editorials in the *Syria Times* pertain to the need for an Arab solution to the Iraqi invasion of Kuwait and preserve Arab unity. However, the newspaper discusses the need for an Arab-solution by presenting an argument that points out how Arabs became divided and could not fight Israeli territorial aggression.

Through micro themes the narrative progresses with Assad-and-Syria-as-peacemakers who call for an Arab-solution requiring Iraq to withdraw and restore the Kuwaiti government so that the Arab Nation can get back to defending itself from the Zionist threat. Israel takes the role in the narrative of the true enemy of the Arabs which takes-advantage of the Arab's division with the help of its ally, the United States. Consequently, the United States is accused of using a double-standard when it deals with the Israelis. Finally, the *Syria Times* calls for Iraq to withdraw from Kuwait and restore the Al-Sabah monarchy so that foreign troops would leave Arab soil and the Arabs could get back to waging the Intifada.

The *Times* calls for immediate withdrawal of Iraq from Kuwait and the restoration of the monarchy as a way to secure Arab unity. Syria and Assad-as-peacemakers theme is again emphasized when Syria calls for an Arab summit (August 5, 1990 "Expression of Arab conscience"). Because Assad represents the broad Arab view that stresses the need for a peaceful Arab solution through an Iraqi withdrawal of invasion forces and the restoration of the Kuwaiti ruler, the editorials express a concern about the Bush and Gorbachev agreement that sanctions the use of force if necessary to accomplish that goal.

Although the newspaper calls for a peaceful Arab solution to the problem of Iraq invading Kuwait, Israel and the Zionist threat to Arab territory predominate each editorial. In its editorial of August 5, 1990 "Expression of Arab conscience," Israel is recognized as the only nation to benefit from the Gulf crisis. And, again on August 16 the *Times* says that Lebanese territorial legitimacy had received a setback because of the crisis (August 16, 1990, "Lebanon:Reforms and by-gone fears"). By as early as September, Iraq's invasion is said to have "stabbed the Intifada in the back"(September 9, 1990 "Difficult questions in difficult times") whereupon Israeli expansionist schemes have been provided a cover for Zionists who want the Gaza Strip(September 27,1990 "The indisputable fact"). In October, the *Times* summarizes Syria's position when it calls for the immediate withdrawal of Iraq from Kuwait and the restoration of the legitimate authority in that country in order to get foreign troops off Arab soil and the Arab community's attention back to the Intifada (October 9, 1990 in the editorial "Basic ingredients at hand").

The double-standard theme is seen throughout the editorials when the *Times* compares the U.S. treatment of Israel and Iraq. After the Al-

Aqsa mosque killings in Israel the *Syria Times,* in an article titled
"Double standard, once again!" asks Americans to "make up their
minds," are they for "right and justice or for aggression?" This editorial
follows the Israeli decision not to let the United Nations investigate the
Al-Aqsa Mosque massacre where several Muslims were killed by Israeli police. The *Times* reminds the reader that the United States, while
condemning Israel for war crimes, proceeds to give them aid in the
form of Patriot missiles, F-15 fighters, and 700-million dollars in military assistance coupled with 400-million dollars to settle Jewish immigrants.

While a peaceful solution among Arabs predominates the dialogue in
the *Times'* editorials, the World community, the United States, and the
U.N. are seen as incapable of solving the problem without using force.
According to the editorials, the escalation of foreign (U.S.) troops and
confrontational forces only serve the enemies of the Arab nation. Saddam Hussein is not discussed as an individual, instead the invasion of
Kuwait by Iraq is discussed as an erroneously ambitious, and foolish act
that can only weaken the Arab cause.

Although the *Times* calls for Iraq's unconditional withdrawal from
Kuwait from the beginning of the crisis, it appeals to all Arabs to join in
Syria's demand(August 5, 1990 in the editorial "Expression of Arab
conscience," August 30, 1990 editorial "Grave and terrifying dangers!"). It becomes immediately apparent that the removal of foreign
troops (U.S.) from Arab soil underlies the *Times'* demand for Iraq's unconditional withdrawal. On August 17, 1990, in the editorial "The
tragic situation must end," the *Times* says that foreign troops are "dag-
gers" to the Arab cause, while foreign ships, in the August 30, 1990 editorial ("Grave and terrible dangers!") are seen as a threat to an Arab
solution. The *Times* editorializes that foreign troops are not in the region to protect Arabs but to play the North against the South (September 2, 1990 editorial, "There is a way out"). The *Times* says that
attention has been drawn away from the Intifada by the Iraqi invasion of
Kuwait, while foreign troops have been allowed to become established
on Middle East soil (October 9, 1990 in the editorial "Basic ingredients
at hand,").

Consequently, the United States is seen as an interventionist power
with a history of backing Syria's enemy, Israel. The double-standard
theme with the United States supporting Israel is brought into a larger
context when the editorials hold the United States directly responsible

for damaging the Arab Nation through its support of Israel. The immigration of Soviet Jews into Israel and, specifically, the Golan Heights with the blessings of the United States, is compared to Iraq's invasion and the settlement of Kuwait. In a December 13, 1990 editorial, "Sabre rattling and wardrums," the *Times* calls upon Iraq to abide by the Cairo summit resolutions and withdraw from Kuwait. At the same time, the *Times* compares Israel which continues to take more Arab land (the Golan Heights) with Iraq whose territorial aggression has made the entire Arab nation a target of oppression.

Conclusion

Major actors in the *Syria Times* editorials for the August, 1990, through December, 1990 pre-war period are, the Arab Nation, Syria and President Assad, Iraq, Israel, and the United States and President Bush. Through these actors macro themes emerge supported by various micro themes.

An Arab solution through Arab-unity with President Assad-as-peacemaker dominates the editorials. Iraq's invasion of Kuwait is seen within the perspective of harming the Arab cause, resulting in a fragmentation of Arab unity and, therefore, endangering the Intifada. Israel, at the same time, is seen as taking advantage of Arab division by increasing settlements and, therefore, endangering territorial integrity of Lebanon, the Gaza Strip, and the Golan Heights.

President Assad emerges as the good Arab who calls for Iraq to withdraw from Kuwait and restore the legitimate government within an Arab solution. Assad's stand is not concerned with the "evil" Saddam Hussein, who is rarely mentioned by name, but, with Israel, which uses this division of Arabs to divert world attention away from the Intifada.

The foreign-troops-on-Arab-soil theme underlies the withdraw-and-restore theme, while the U.S.-as-interventionist theme is linked with the foreign-troops-on-Arab-soil theme. Under the double-standard theme the *Times* equates Israel with the United States and points out that the U.S.-Israeli collusion is a threat to Arab unity and an equitable and just solution of the Israeli-Palestinian problem.

Through the narrative of macro and micro themes, the Arab Nation becomes the victim in the Gulf crisis. The *Times* is concerned that Iraqi aggression has diverted attention away from the Intifada and damaged the Arab cause. The United States, because of its alliance with Israel is seen as an aggressor and an interventionist, while the Arab Nation, Syria, and Assad, become peacemakers through an Arab solution.

Macro and Micro Themes

Arab-Unity
   Assad-and-Syria-as-peacemakers
   Arab-solution
   Withdraw-and-restore
Arab-Division
   Iraq-hurts-Arab-cause
   Israel-takes-advantage
   U.S.-as-Israel's-ally
   Double-standard
   U.S.-as-interventionist
   Foreign-troops-on-Arab-soil
   Intifada-interrupted
   Zionist-threat-to-Arabs

The Arab News, *Saudi Arabia*

In the *Arab News,* for the pre-war and war period, August, 1990 through February, 1991, analysis revealed four macro themes that dominated the editorials. The Arab-unity theme dominated throughout the editorials, however, at the same time, the *Arab News* shifted responsibility for solving the problem of the Iraqi invasion of Kuwait to the united international community from the Arab Nation, thus creating a world-unity theme. Other macro themes played an important part in the discussion. The no-linkage theme dealt with Israel and the Palestinian issue, while the Saddam Hussein-as-aggressor/Hitler theme provided the *Arab News* and the world community with an appropriate villain in the war narrative.

Analysis also revealed that several actors played well defined roles in the war narrative. These consisted of organizational actors;the United Nations, and the PLO. Then there are nation states, as well as individual leaders, as actors such as, Kuwait, Iraq, Saudi Arabia, Israel, and the United States, King Fahd, Saddam Hussein, and George Bush.

Arab-Unity

Analysis revealed that the Arab-unity theme and a peaceful Arab so-lution to the problem of Iraq invading Kuwait soon crumbled in the edi-torials. Several micro themes contributed to the newspaper turning over the solution of Iraq invading Kuwait to the world community. These include, the Arabs-divided theme, the Kuwait-as-victim theme, the Saudi Arabia-as-potential-victim theme, and the withdraw-and-restore theme.

While the Arabs sought a peaceful solution in the beginning of the time period, it became apparent quite early that the Arabs could not pre-sent a united front. The Arab Nation thus, became divided according to the *Arab News*, and must look to the international community for pro-tection against a fellow Arab nation, Iraq. Throughout the discussion covering the seven-month time span, Saddam Hussein is not only seen as the reason for this division, but he is also presented as the aggressor, as a Hitler whose actions (the Iraqi invasion of Kuwait) have dealt a major blow to the Palestinian cause. Also, the micro theme of with-draw-and-restore places the monarchy of Kuwait, the Al-Sabah family, and Saudi Arabia, as a neighboring sheikhdom, as potential victims of Saddam's aggressions.

The United States' presence in Saudi Arabia is explained as a defen-sive measure through which the Arab nation would have time to solve the Iraqi invasion of Kuwait through various summits. While the inva-sion of Kuwait is seen as a transgression of one Arab upon another, Ku-wait is glorified as the good Arab who "raises the poor," while contributing to other Arab countries. Iraq is described as violating Ku-wait in a "blitzkrieg of aggression," whereby Arab unity is broken through the "most hideous crime" of an Arab brother violating another. The *Arab News* thus, established the call for Iraq to withdraw from Ku-wait and restore the Kuwaiti monarchy (August 9, 1990, in "days of an-guish").

The invasion of Kuwait quickly becomes a world issue early in the pre-war period. Editorials in August discuss two specific events which placed the invasion in the international arena, namely, the Gulf Co-op-eration Council (GCC) meeting in Jeddah(August 9, 1990 in "Days of anguish"), and the Cairo summit, discussed as a last chance for an Arab solution (August 10, 1990 in "Last chance"). A meeting where Mubarak of Egypt and King Fahd agreed that the Iraqi invasion of Kuwait was a direct blow to the Palestinian cause was also discussed in the August 10, 1990 editorial.

The *News* compares Saddam to Chengiz Khan, Stalin, and Hitler and states that his action forced the issue into the world arena, and the world community must defend the oil states against this "shrewd, cold-blooded megalomaniac." The United Nations is urged to take action and the foreign-troops-defend-Arab soil theme enters as a micro theme (August 13, 1990 "Bullying the world").

World-Unity Theme

Analysis revealed that the *Arab News* turned to the world community early in the crisis, to solve the problem of Saddam Hussein invading Kuwait. Thus the world-unity theme became apparent early in the time period supported by several micro themes, such as, the world-responsibility, foreign-troops-defend-Arab-soil, the U.S.-defends-Arabs, and peace-through-force.

In an editorial on September 11, 1990 titled "The summit," the *Arab News* discussed the meeting between the United States and the Soviet Union that resulted in a consensus against Saddam Hussein. George Bush and Mikhael Gorbachev emerged in the editorial as strengthening the resolve of the international community for unconditional withdrawal, restoration of the legitimate government of Kuwait, and the release of "hostages"(foreigners detained by Saddam in Iraq). Although Arab unity remains an important part of the Saudi dialogue, attention quickly turns to U.N. resolutions, the embargo, and the resolution of the conflict through an international consensus.

An analysis of various nations' participation in the world-unity theme is based, not only upon the world's obligation and willingness to fight a world tyrant, but, also, on economic issues. Gorbachev is seen as trading his support for cash (September 11, 1990, "The summit"), while NATO is seen as a powerless body with the European community in economic disarray (on October 16, 1990, "Beyond NATO"). In this editorial, the United States is seen as a buffer which is in need of financial support for its military, one that is in Saudi Arabia primarily to defend that country against an invasion by Saddam Hussein. This editorial runs through a list of European countries: Germany is powerless to send troops but can send money, Italy is "standoffish," the French are "above the crowd," but Margaret Thatcher is unique in her "solo flight into heroism" for sending troops to the Gulf.

An interesting theme emerging in the editorials is peace-through-force. Iraq was given a January-15 deadline by the United Nations to withdraw from Kuwait and essentially capitulate to the allied forces. The editorials at this time shifted responsibility to Saddam Hussein to meet the demands of the international community with no concessions. After the bombing began on January 15, the editorials of the *Arab News* placed the obligation for a peaceful resolution that could save Iraq's people, squarely upon Saddam Hussein.

Equally important, negotiations on the part of Saudi Arabia to pay for the troop buildup are not discussed in the editorials of this time period. Oil, a theme that could be expected to dominate the discussion, is rarely mentioned.

Saddam Hussein-As-Aggressor/Hitler

While Saddam-as-aggressor/Hitler theme is a macro theme, several micro themes contribute to Saddam Hussein's demonization in the war narrative. Analysis revealed that the micro-themes, such as, remember-the-1930s, the Saddam-as-bad-Arab, and Saddam-is-responsible emerged in the editorials.

The remember-the-1930s theme constantly reminded the readers of decisions made by world leaders to grant concessions to Hitler in the early part of his blitzkrieg leading to World War II. The appeasement of Hitler in 1938 at Munich is first mentioned when British Foreign Secretary Douglas Hurd raised questions concerning the Soviet Union, a member of the international community, which was opposed to military measures to get Iraq out of Kuwait. The *News* consequently warns that, "This means that the fight against Hitlers should start with a fight against Chamberlains (British) and Daladiers (French) in our midst" (September 9, 1990, in "Moscow and the Gulf crisis"). Throughout the remaining time periods the remember-the-1930s theme made intermittent appearances. The *Arab News* says that the "World" was responsible for World War II through appeasement of a similar tyrant (Hitler) in Munich in the 1930s (September 17, 1990, in "Time for reflection"). Czechoslovakia is also equated with Kuwait in more than one editorial (September 24, 1990, in "A generous gesture"). Mussolini's 1935 attack against Abyssinia is compared to Iraq's invasion of Kuwait. The *Arab News* reminds the world community, through warnings to the United Nations, that the appeasement of Mussolini in the 1930s spelled the end of the League of Nations as a major factor in international relations. Consequently, appeasement of Saddam Hussein, a modern-day dictator, would surely lead to the end of the United Nations (November 1, 1990, in "From Abyssinia to Kuwait").

While care is taken not to personally attack Saddam Hussein in the early editorials after the invasion and before the Cairo (Arab) summit, Saddam is compared to Hitler from the middle of August and the comparisons continue throughout the pre-war and war periods. In an early editorial, Saddam is described as an evil dictator who sacrifices his own people while raping, looting, and killing an oppressed fellow Arab country (August 13, 1990, in "Bullying the world").

After the Cairo summit, the invasion of Kuwait by Iraq is seen by the *Arab News* as a problem that the world cannot ignore. A multinational army and navy are justified to rescue Kuwait and contain Iraq which "violates civilized norms of behavior" thereby wounding the Arab "family" (August 12, 1990, in "As flotillas converge"). Baghdad's aggression is called worse than Hitler's because Iraq has invaded an unsuspecting Arab neighbor which is "tiny, rich, and generous." In mid August, the *Arab News* also refers to Saddam resorting to the "law of the jungle," whereby a stronger neighbor devours its smaller prey (August 16, 1990, in "Monstrous"). Hence, Saudi Arabia-as-a-potential-victim theme rationalizes the presence of foreign troops on Saudi soil, because only the world community can stop this ruthless and villainous transgressor.

After the Helsinki summit in September, when President Bush and Gorbachev backed the United Nations air embargo of Iraq, the analysis of Saddam Hussein continued. The *Arab News* accuses Saddam of violating civilized norms through murder and plunder in Kuwait, thus diverting attention away from the Palestinian cause (September 27, 1990, in "The resolve strengthens"). These actions not only led to further erosion of Palestinian rights, but inspired the Zionists to kill moslems at the Al-Aqsa mosque (October 10, 1990, in "Al-Aqsa). The *News* further discusses King Fahd's call for the restoration of the Kuwaiti monarchy and continues to compare Saddam Hussein's invasion of Kuwait to Hitler's war of aggrandizement (December 6, 1990, in "War or Peace?"). By January, 1991, Hussein is seen as a war criminal who is responsible for Iraqi civilian deaths as air raids are continued by allied forces (January 22, 1991, in "POWS in Iraq").

No-Linkage Theme

The no-linkage theme is supported through various micro themes that recur throughout the pre-war and war periods. Thus, while the newspaper equates Kuwaitis with the Palestinians in an attempt to bring the invasion into the world arena, it denies any linkage professed by Saddam Hussein. In a careful analysis of Saddam's attempt to "link" the issue of Israel's occupation of Palestinian territory to Iraq's invasion of Kuwait, the *Arab News* suggests that Saddam has done damage to the Arab Nation that is equal to what Israel has done, and that Israel is the only regional actor to benefit from Iraq's actions.

At the same time, however, it is apparent that the *Arab News* approaches this issue with caution. The Israeli-Palestinian issue is first mentioned in the August 9, 1990 ("Days of anguish"), when the Iraqi invasion is said to divide Arabs who had otherwise been united in working toward a solution to the Palestinian issue. The Israel-benefits theme is developed a little later when Saddam Hussein is said to be Israel's savior who "stabs Palestinians in the back" by diverting world attention away from the Palestinian issue (August 11, 1990, "Moral wrong knows no boundaries"). Accordingly, the world's attention is drawn to the similarities of Israel's territorial claims to disputed Palestinian lands and Iraq's claims to Kuwait. Again, in September, Saddam Hussein is equated with Israel through his "colonization" of Kuwait (September 18, 1990, in "A leaf out of Israel's book").

Reference to Israel in the editorials is noticeably sparse until October 10, 1990 when the Al-Aqsa mosque killings prompted a discussion that blamed Saddam Hussein for the example he set. Saddam Hussein is said to have deviated from civilized norms, and, by killing the Palestinian peace process, has allowed Israel to benefit from the crisis. On October 26, 1990 in an editorial ("Israel's intransigence"), the *Arab News* says that Israel's refusal to allow a U.N. mission into Israel to investigate the mosque killings benefits Saddam Hussein by giving him a chance to break down the world consensus.

Conclusion

Analysis of the actors and themes over the seven-month period, August, 1990 through February, 1991 revealed that the Arab Nation, King Fahd, the international community, the United Nations, the United States and President Bush, Saddam Hussein, Kuwait, and Israel are major actors. Macro themes include the following: Arab-Unity, World-Unity, Saddam-as-aggressor (Hitler), and no-linkage. Not unlike the actors whose actions form the macro themes, the micro themes revolve around the actions and history of various actors. These micro themes include, remember-the-1930s, foreign-troops-defend-Arab-soil, withdraw-and-restore, Saddam-as-bad-Arab, Saudi Arabia-as-potential-victim, and Palestine-and-Kuwait-are-world-issues.

The themes appear to be numerous and varied, but in actuality, they fit neatly into the narrative of the text. Iraq, and especially Saddam Hussein, is labeled very early as the aggressor, and is demonized through the Saddam-as-Hitler macro theme which is supported by various micro themes. Accordingly, Arab unity is the first victim of Iraq's aggression. This aggression is promptly linked with and compared to Israeli aggression on the Palestinians. Saddam Hussein, of course, bears the direct responsibility to solve the problem by heeding the warnings of the world community and unconditionally withdrawing from Kuwait and restoring the legitimate Al-Sabah monarchy to power.

In the editorials, the *Arab News* associates Saudi Arabia with Kuwait as a victim, which, therefore, justifies allowing foreign troops on Arab soil. According to the editorials, these foreign troops (primarily U.S.) serve two functions, 1). they defend Saudi Arabia from invasion of Saddam Hussein's army, and 2). they allow the World community to defend Saudi Arabia and solve the problem with the United States acting within United Nations and, therefore, a world consensus.

Major actors played clearly defined roles in the war narrative that was presented by the *Arab News*. Saddam Hussein was clearly the aggressor, while the United States became the enforcer with the United Nations as the peacemaker. The Arab Nation, including Kuwait and Saudi Arabia, soon became the major victim through the aggression of a wayward Arab brother, Saddam Hussein. Saddam Hussein was immediately demonized through comparisons with Hitler and other fascist dictators of the 1930s, while Israel, the Arab Nation's long-established enemy, was equated with Iraq through a comparison of their policies of territorial aggression.

Macro and Micro Themes

Arab-Unity
   Arabs-divided
   Kuwait-as-victim

   Saudi Arabia-as-potential-victim
   Withdraw-and-restore
World-unity
   World-responsibility
   Foreign-troops-defend-Arab-soil
   U.S.-defends-Arabs
   Peace-through-force
No-linkage
   Saddam-equals-Israel
   Palestine-and-Kuwait-are-world-issues
   Israel-benefits
Saddam Hussein-as-aggressor/Hitler
   Remember-the-1930s
   Saddam-as-bad-Arab
   Saddam-responsible

The United Arab Emirates News

   Editorials in the *United Arab Emirates News* concerning the Persian
Gulf crisis and war appeared everyday over the seven-month period,
from August, 1990 through February, 1991. The editorial section contained editorials from five Arabic language Emirate newspapers, Al
Bayan, Al Ittihad, Al Fajr, Al Wahda, and Al Khaleej. These editorials
were relatively short and diversified in number, with as few as one per
day to as many as four editorials on another day. In 164 days, during
the pre-war period the *UAE News* contained 416 editorials, while during
the war period the daily published 137 editorials on 48 days. The days
with editorials including the pre-war and war periods numbered 202 for
a total of 553 separate editorials. An analysis of the various combina-
tions of editorials from the five Emirates revealed a repitition of themes
among the editorials. Most editorials were reactions to one of many
Arab meetings, or an attempt to tie Shiekh Zayed and the United Arab
Emirates to the Arab Nation and the International community in justifying war.
   The *Emirate News* for the seven-month time period, contained a sim-
plistic discussion of actors. Hence, themes were developed through
these actors with little discussion or counter-discussion of the history of
the region. Analysis of the text provided opinions that appeared to be
rather pliable and subject to change depending on the direction of the

political wind in spite of hyperbole demonstrated by the contributing editors.

Analysis revealed three macro themes that dominated the war narrative in the *UAE News*. Each of the three macro themes, Arab-unity, the International-community-as peacemaker, and the Saddam-as-greedy-aggressor, was supported by micro themes that presented a very clear war narrative.

Arab-Unity

Several micro themes contributed to the Arab-unity theme. Sheikh Zayed-as-the-wise-leader emerged early in the time period when the editorials called for a peaceful-Arab-solution to what was considered, in the beginning of the time period, an inter-Arab problem. However, the Arabs were soon divided by the linkage issue when Iraq tried to link the Palestinian/Israeli issue to its invasion of Kuwait. While the no-linkage micro theme seemed to explain why a peaceful Arab solution was not forthcoming in the crisis, the sudden massing of international troops in Saudi Arabia made it necessary to look to the international community to solve, what the *News* primarily considered an inter-Arab problem.

The Arab Unity theme predominated from the beginning of the crisis with Sheikh Zayed-as-the-wise-leader theme reinforcing Arab Unity. Various actors, Egypt, Syria, and the Palestinians, are seen as having their own opinions and stakes within the Arab Unity theme. Although the Arab Nation's primary interest had been to solve the Israeli-Palestinian issue, the *Emirate News* is careful in not playing up the issue. Iraq, on the other hand, forces the issue through the linkage theme. Iraq wants to negotiate its withdrawal from Kuwait with stipulations demanding world attention in solving the Palestinian-Israeli issue. An ongoing discussion at various Arab summits concerning where each Arab Nation stood in relation to the question of linkage provides an arena in which the Arabs were able to participate in the inter-Arab dialogue on the crisis. In the final analysis, each calls for Iraq to withdraw from Kuwait thereby denying Iraq linkage as a negotiating tool. Israel-benefits-from-inter-Arab conflict is a theme contained in editorials beginning as early as August, 1990 and continues through the discussion of linkage of the Palestinian issue with Iraq's invasion of Kuwait. Although the no-linkage theme is not a major one in the editorials it does run as a minor theme throughout the period. On September 19, 1990, Israel and Iraq are compared. The *Emirate News* draws parallels between the

Iraqi territorial disputes and its policies of population resettlement and the Israeli territorial disputes and its "practices in the West Bank and Gaza Strip." Although Israel is seen as an enemy of the Arab Nation throughout the time period, the *Emirate News* refuses to recognize the linkage as a legitimate issue. It recognizes the heroic struggle of the Palestinians against Israel, yet, it does not want to link it to Saddam Hussein (December 9, 1990).

International-Community-as-Peacemaker Theme

The international-community-as-peacemaker theme was supported by several micro themes. Multi-national-forces-protect-Arabs, the Bush-as-enforcer, the U.S.=world=U.N., and the unconditional-with-draw-and-restore themes contributed to the International-community-as-peacemaker theme.

Although Iraq's invasion is seen by the *Emirate News* as a mere "rift" among the Arab brotherhood in the beginning of August, the invasion soon takes on an Iraq-against-the-world tone. The world unity theme runs through the editorials and the interest of the international community encompassing the United Nations, the United States, and the Arab Nation to reverse the invasion is emphasized. The United Arab Emirates with Sheikh Zayed as its wise leader is said to represent the interest of the Arab Nation.

In an August 11, 1990 editorial, the *Emirate News* discusses the opportunity for an Arab solution. Editorials in the *Emirate News* for the two or three days surrounding the Cairo summit discussed various issues, such as, Kuwait as a victim, foreign troops protecting Arabs, and the effectiveness of sanctions against Iraq. By September 1, 1990, editorials turned the focus to the U.N. with Secretary-General Javier Perez de Cuellar the defender of an Arab solution within the International community. In an editorial as early as August 26, 1990, the *Emirate News* discussed the Soviet Union joining the international community by appealing to Saddam Hussein to abide by the Security Council's resolution to withdraw. The Helsinki summit, discussed in editorials on September 11, 1990 further linked the United States and the Soviet Union in a common bond to enforce norms and legitimacy set by international law.

The United States, however, is not mentioned in the context of the foreign-troops theme. Foreign troops were referred to as multi-national forces which included Arab troops, thereby adding to the legitimacy needed for the presence of foreign troops on Arab soil.

In an October editorial, the *UAE News* discussed the need for a peaceful solution with France not wanting war and Italy warning Iraq not to attack Israel. While these actors were mentioned briefly, the bulk of the discussion concerning the international community focused on the Soviet Union, the United States, and the United Nations.

Saddam-as-Greedy-Aggressor

Analysis revealed that Saddam became the greedy aggressor early in the editorials. The hostage theme, Kuwait-as-victim theme, and the Arab-Nation-as-victim theme made Saddam responsible for international action against Iraq, and justified the newspaper's call for Saddam to withdraw and avert the destruction of his own people.

The Iraqi-greed theme and Iraq-as-the-aggressor theme dominated the editorials beginning of September and ran through the entire time period. However, it is interesting to remember that in the immediate aftermath of Iraq's invasion of Kuwait, the problem was seen as merely a rift among Arabs. Consequently, as soon as the international community entered the discussion, taking the solution away from the Arabs, Iraq was said to have committed an "unprecedented crime" against Kuwait and the Iraqi people.

The multi-national-forces-protect-Arabs theme also began to appear early in the editorials, as a protection against Iraq. The unconditional-withdraw-and-restore (monarchy) theme dominated as the *Emirate News* repeated the allegations of Iraqi war crimes enumerating mass killings, expulsions, and arrests of Kuwaitis (October 5, 1990). Subsequently, the *Emirate News* editorials, in defense of Kuwaiti monarchy, discussed the Al Sabah family and their pledge for more democracry for the Kuwaiti people (October 13, 1990).

The hostage theme, while never developed into a major theme, depicted Iraq as an insincere negotiator for peace. Iraq's promise to release the hostages was seen a play for time (November 22, 1990). And, by December, editorials denied that the release of the hostages was a humanitarian gesture and reaffirmed the world's resolve to force Iraq to withdraw from Kuwait and restore its Emir (December 9, 1990). By January 1991, the *Emirate News* appealed to Iraq to withdraw, restore, and avert the destruction that was sure to follow the military action of the allied forces, because they would surely "defeat the evil

hands that have desecrated a holy and beloved land." Two weeks before the countdown for the January 15, 1991 deadline for Iraq to unconditionally withdraw from Kuwait began, Saddam Hussein was seen by
the *Emirate News* as an arrogant criminal who was willing to sacrifice
the people of Iraq for his own greed (January 1, 1991). From January 1
through the end of the war period, the editorials continued to call upon
Saddam to withdraw and avert the destruction of his own people. After
the bombing began on January 16, 1991 editorials reminded readers that
there was still time for Saddam to avert the destruction of Iraq and
shifted the blame for the bombing to Saddam Hussein and the Saddam-
is-responsible theme began.

The editorials also depicted the United States, with President Bush as
its steadfast leader, as the enforcer of the international community's
will. President Bush, by rejecting any conditions for Iraq's withdrawal
from Kuwait was said, by the newspaper, to be rightfully denying Iraq
any reward for its crimes.

Editorials in the *Emirate News* after the bombing of Iraq began to appeal to Iraq to withdraw, not only to save Iraq, but, to prevent a global
war (February 3, 1991). By February 26, 1991, the newspaper pro-
claimed a victory for the world while calling for Saddam Hussein to be
punished. "Desert Storm" was said to be "blowing on Kuwait to uproot
aggression" while the Iraqi people and its army have paid the price of
Saddam Hussein's arrogance.

Conclusion

Analysis of the many editorials in the *United Arab Emirate News*
over the pre-war and war period revealed a war narrative created by a
limited number of actors. Major actors were Iraq as the aggressor, and
Sheikh Zayed, the United Arab Emirates, the Arab Nation and the International Community under the umbrella of the United Nations as peacemakers. Kuwait and the Arabs were seen as victims, and the United
States, with George Bush as its leader, became the enforcer.

Various major and minor themes developed that supported the actors
and their roles within the narrative. The Arab-unity theme was sub-
sumed under the world-unity theme. Sheikh Zayed, at the same time,
maintained the position of the wise-Arab-leader through various meetings with leaders of the international community and non-Arab Muslim
leaders.

Saddam Hussein-as-greedy-aggressor became a theme early in the *Emirate News* editorials. The Saddam-as-greedy-aggressor theme gave rise to the withdraw-and-avert theme through which the editorials held Saddam Hussein responsible for the massive bombings and the short, but devastating ground war that followed. During the war period, the themes that emerged were: Saddam-is-responsible, Saddam-the-greedy-aggressor, and George Bush-the-enforcer.

Analysis of the editorials, should not only consider the themes emphasised, but, the themes iqnored in the text. For instance, the control of oil and the inter-Arab conflict that the regional leaders were experiencing during their many meetings should have been of particular interest to the newspaper's readers. Through pointed commissions and ommissions the *Emirate News* tells the story of a nation that is caught in a very precarious position in the Middle East community of nations. The language used in the editorials is filled with hyperbole and rhetoric that carefully tries to glorify actions that defend its own precarious standing among Arabs and Muslims. While the U.A.E. has many of the characteristics of Kuwait, analysis revealed that the *UAE News* fully understood the power of Iraq in the hierarchy of states in the Middle East.

Macro and Micro Themes

Arab Unity
    Zayed-as-wise-leader
    Arab-solution-peaceful
    No-linkage-Isreali-Palestinian-issue
    Israel-benefits
International-community-as-peacemaker
    Multi-national Forces protect Arabs
    Bush-as-enforcer
    U.S.=World=U.N.
    Unconditional-withdraw-and-restore
 Saddam-as-greedy-aggressor
    Saddam-responsible
    Withdraw-and-avert
    Kuwait-as-victim
    Arab-Nation-as-Victim
    Hostage

The Jerusalem Post

Editorials in the *Post* for the pre-war and war period of August, 1990, through February, 1991, totaled 105. Specifically, the pre-war period contained 75 editorials, while the war period contained 30 editorials. On most days, the *Post* ran a single editorial, except for a few double subject entries.

Analysis of editorials in the *Jerusalem Post* for the time periods reveals macro and micro themes concerning the issue of Iraq's invasion of Kuwait the day after the invasion beginning on August 3, 1990. Major state actors include, Iraq, Jordan, Syria, Saudi Arabia, France, Britain, Germany, Japan, the Soviet Union, and, the United States, while the organizational actors include, the PLO, and the United Nations. Individual actors include leaders, such as, Saddam Hussein, President George Bush, and Yasir Arafat. The *Post's* discussion of these actors provides a wide variety of themes, both macro and micro, throughout the time period. Each macro theme is supported by an interlacing of micro themes.

Saddam-As-Hitler/Aggressor

Saddam Hussein-as-aggressor/Hitler/dictator is supported by micro themes, such as, remember-the-1930's, democracies-versus-totalitarian dictatorship, and arm-democracies-only. The progression of themes, on the other hand, leads to and supports the macro theme the-world-against-Israel.

From the beginning, the editorials compare Saddam Hussein to Hitler, the aggressor. In an editorial on August 3, 1990 (titled "The anschluss"), the size of Israel within the 1967 boundary lines is compared to Kuwait. Saddam Hussein is immediately equated with Hitler who operated as a deliberate aggressor under the facade of the classical "anschluss" or puppet government. Territory and oil are seen as the goals of this aggression as Saddam is placed as the primary threat to the Arab Nation.

While discussing Saddam-as-Hitler, the *Post's* editorials refer to the 1930s, a time when concessions made to Hitler by Britain and France led to further aggression by the dictator. During the first month of the crisis, the use of gas in Nazi death camps is discussed and Saddam Hussein's chemical capabilities are mentioned (August 19, 1990, in

"Deterrers and abetters"). Saddam is said to "rape" Kuwait, the victim(September 19, 1990, in "The challenge of Rosh Hashana"). The *Post* places Israel in the context of the 1930's dislocation of Jews, and, at the same time, comdemns the Palestinians for supporting Iraq in its territorial dispute. Thus, Saddam is said to be a hero to the Palestinians because he is using Palestinians to enforce population transfers in Kuwait (September 19, 1990, in "Palestinizing Kuwait"). Mention is also made of the gassing of Kurds in Iraq by Saddam Hussein. This type of demonizing of Saddam Hussein through the Saddam-as-Hitler theme, with immediate reference to methods used by fascist dictators in the 1930s, followed by characterizing the Palestinians in general, and the PLO specifically, as willful players in Saddam's aggressive territorial plot, unmistakably identifies Israel's real and immediate enemy, the PLO.

World-Against-Israel

Analysis of various arguments presented in each commentary reveals that actors and themes play roles in the conflict depending upon Israel's position during the time period. The Post, in its editorials, gives little discussion to the crisis as a world issue except to call upon the world community to come to the defense of Israel which is the victim in the crisis. The newspaper presents a discussion that shows the world-against-Israel in most matters, especially the Palestinian/Israeli issue. This narrative involved several micro themes that contributed to the image of Israel as a misunderstood nation in the world arena. The micro themes, no-international conference, no-linkage, PLO-terrorists, and PLO-against-Palestinians helped weave an image of Israel that eventually led to both Middle Eastern countries and members of the world community being classified as friends or enemies of Israel.

The *Post* begins the world-against-Israel theme in the first days of the period by blaming Kuwait, the United Arab Emirates, and Saudi Arabia for Iraq's military buildup during the Iran-Iraq war (August 3, 1990 "The anschluss"). Saddam is equated with Assad of Syria, Gaddafi of Libya, and is placed as a dictator who is only interested in territory. According to the editorial, the United States is the only country which is powerful enough to force Iraq out of Kuwait.

Reaction to Mikhail Gorbachev's request for an international conference to solve the Palestinian-Israeli issue, at the Helsinki summit in September, along with President Bush's reported favorable consideration of the possibility of the conference, began the micro theme no-international conference that would continue throughout the crisis. In September, an international conference is first mentioned in relation to the Persian Gulf crisis when the newspaper establishes the world-against-Israel theme by discussing Israel as a victim of the international community which is vying for allies among the Arab countries at Israel's cost. Syria, Egypt, and Saudi Arabia are seen to benefit from the proposed conference, while the United States is seen as trading international visibility of the issue to gain Arab allies (September 12, 1991, in "American retreat").

In October, 1990 reaction by the *Post* to the United Nation's request to send an investigative team into Israel to examine the circumstances surrounding the killing of 17 Palestinians on the Temple Mount in Jerusalem by Israeli police, further solidified the no-international-conference theme, the Israel-misunderstood theme, and the PLO-as-terrorists theme. On October 10, 1990, in the editorial "Handing out blame," world response to the Temple Mount "tragedy" is discussed as "outrageous" by the *Post*. The editorial asks why the United Nations singles out Israel which has merely "quelled the riot" of premeditated, and "purposeful violence" against Jews by the PLO, while Saudi Arabia killed 402 pilgrims in three hours of rioting in Mecca in 1987, and democracies such as the United States, India, and Venezuela have killed hundreds of unarmed rioters in the past with no subsequent U.N. action. Israel, as a democracy, has the right to defend itself, according to the editorial, from the terrorist, (rock throwing) actions of the PLO. The incident is further linked in the editorial to the Persian Gulf crisis as being an effort by the PLO to deflect attention away from the crisis and direct it to the Palestinian issue.

Implicit in this view in the *Post* editorials is the assumption that Israel is alone in its ability to understand what protective measures are needed concerning the Palestinians, and, therefore, Arabs in general. Four days after the October 10 editorial, on October 14, 1990, in an editorial titled "A risk that Israel cannot take," the *Post* challenges the United States for backing the U.N. decision to send a mission to Israel to investigate the killings. The United States is accused by the *Post* of "placating the Arabs" to gain the support of the anti-Saddam coalition among the Arab countries. The United States, in this instance, is equated with Britain which, according to the editorials, in the 1930s "placated" the Arabs by adopting various restrictive measures, including, restricting Jewish immigration to Palestine, even though the Arab regimes at the time were sympathetic to the Nazis. From this point in the pre-war period macro themes support one another in an interlacing of such themes as Israel-against-the-world, Israel-misunderstood, Saddam-equals-Hitler, democracies-defend-with weapons, totalitarian regimes/dictators-oppress, and the PLO-are-terrorists.

Friends-And-Enemies-Of-Israel

Analysis of the *Post's* editorials revealed a well developed friends-and-enemies-of-Israel theme that included both Arabs and the international community. A number of minor themes may be identified in the editorials, themes such as the double-standard, no-linkage (an effort to deny the Israeli-Palestinian issue to be linked with Saddam Hussein's invasion of Kuwait), Bad-Arabs, Good-Arabs, and the PLO-as-terrorists, support the friends-and-enemies-of-Israel, etc. There are also some major and minor actors of different categories, such as, Saddam Hussein, Arab nations, European nations, the United States, the PLO, and the United Nations. In the editorials, the *Post* subsequently divides the world community into the enemies of Israel(those who want linkage), and, the United States, the ally, which is also the guarantor of world peace.

Early in the period, the United States is again called upon to settle the dispute as the list of Arab countries having involvement with Saddam. The Arab Nation is seen as divided and not capable of solving its own problems. The *Post* also editorializes on a range of issues, such as, the PLO helps Saddam, Saddam bludgeons Kuwait, Saudi Arabia cannot resort to old methods of paying Hussein off, the Saudis taking an appropriate decision in allowing foreign troop buildup on its own soil. It also praises the Saudi and Turkish decision to close the Iraqi oil pipeline (August 9, 1990, in "America wakes up").

Jordan, Syria, and Saudi Arabia are given considerable attention from the *Post* throughout both time periods creating the bad-Arab theme. Editorials presented a constant evaluation of where these nations stood not only in relation to, Saddam Hussein, but, their contribution to the Israeli-Palestinian conflict.

Jordan is accused of being the instigator of the Temple Mount killings to take the focus off the Gulf and put it on Israel. Yet, while discussion of the push by the United States for observers in Israel is seen as the United States playing into Arab hands, it is evident that the Israelis count on the United States supporting the Israeli position (December 12, 1990, in "playing Saddam's game").

Financial compensation to Arab allies in the coalition against Saddam Hussein is a constant theme beginning in August and continuing throughout the seven-month period. The *Post's* discussion of Jordan and Syria becomes especially heated in the three weeks preceding the January 15 deadline for Iraq to withdraw from Kuwait. During this period the *Post* editorials suggested that since Jordan, under King Hussein, was in association with the terrorist PLO, it simply could not be trusted (December 19, 1990, in "Koch's choice," January 3, 1991, in "The Fatah anniversary," January 7, 1991, "Jordan's choice," & January 24, 1991, in "Reassuring King Hussein"). In the editorials, the *Post* refers to the international community's request for Israel not to retaliate against possible Iraqi missile attacks if and when the attack takes place.

At the same time, Syria is discussed in the *Post* editorials as a terrorist nation which cannot be trusted in the coalition against Saddam. By the end of November, during talks between President Assad of Syria and President Bush, the editorials warn President Bush that his proposed ally is actually a "territorial bully." Starting in November, Assad is equated with Stalin and Hitler. Under the remember-the-1930s theme the *Post* equates the Iraqi invasion of Kuwait with the invasion of Czechoslovakia by Hitler (November 22, 1990, in "Mr. Bush's ally"). The *Post* describes Assad as a terrorist equal to Stalin who cannot be placated into a true alliance with the coalition of nations against Saddam Hussein (November 28, 1990, in "Raising the heat in Lebanon").

More To The Friends-And-Enemies-Of-Israel Theme

There were other themes throughout the time period, namely, democracies-versus-totalitarian dictatorships, with Israel the only democracy in the conflict zone;the withdraw-and-prevent theme that came into play as the January 15 deadline drew near; the where's-the-money-for-restraint theme where Israel needed money to survive within a war context; and the Arab-unity-threatened theme whereby Saddam Hussein and his alliance with the PLO is seen as a threat to the Arab nations.

By September, 1990, the International community, its actions concerning the crisis and especially linkage of Saddam's invasion with the Palestinian issue, take on the Enemies-of-Israel theme. France, which has helped Iraq with its nuclear power program, is seen as weak for negotiating separately for the release of French "hostages" in Iraq, while maintaining its connection with Arafat and the PLO (September 4, 1990, in "Plus ca change"). After the Helsinki summit, the U.S.-as-enforcer theme is established through Gorbachev's hesitation to take a firm stand against linkage of the Palestinian issue to Saddam's invasion (September 10, 1990, in "Summit in the clouds"). And, in November, Mitterrand of France is discussed by the *Post* as willing to compromise while Egypt refuses to compromise on the linkage issue. In November, the *Post* also reaffirms the no-linkage stand when Saddam Hussein and the PLO are said to be the only ones to benefit from bringing up the Temple-Mount Mosque riots. In the editorials the *Post* emphasizes the fact that Saddam Hussein has diverted attention away from his invasion onto the Israeli/Palestinian issue (November 4, 1990, in "Dangerous linkage").

On January 1, 1991, Bush is advised, by the *Post*, to take a strong stand in his position that Iraq must withdraw from Kuwait with no compromise. The European community is seen as weak and as enemies of Israel because they (Luxembourg and Belgium) said that they will deal with the Palestinian issue if Saddam withdraws (in "European folly"). Germany is said to be the most greedy, callous, and cynical member of the European community which has contributed to Iraq's buildup of biological weapons and missile systems which Saddam Hussein may use against the Israeli people (January 25, 1991, in "German responsibility"). With the bombing of Iraq well underway, the United Nations and particularly UN Secretary-General Javier Perez de Cuellar, is seen by the *Post* as bending to Yemen and Cuba in calling for a cease fire. The Soviet Union, Syria, Iran, Saudi Arabia, the Gulf Emirates, France, Germany, Italy, and Turkey are said to be weak because they do not want to see Iraq destroyed. The United States is again called upon to resist the pressure for a cease fire, and go beyond forcing the withdrawal of Iraq from Kuwait, and destroy the Iraqi military (February 11, 1991, in "Excluding Israel").

The Double-Standard Theme

The *Post* uses an interesting twist to the double-standard theme that is different from what the Arab newspapers professed. In the September 27,1990 editorial "Palestinizing Kuwait," the *Post* accuses Saddam Hussein of transferring populations within Kuwait in order to "Palestinize" it. It also advocates self determination for the Kurds in Iraq by arguing that by virtue of their history and distinctive culture, the Kurds

deserve a separate state of their own, but the West, sadly, has systemati-
cally betrayed the Kurds. By contrast, the Palestinians could live in any
Arab country, including Kuwait, and blend with the local population
without a trace of distinctiveness because of similar language, religion,
and ethnic background. The *Post* marveled at the double standard of
the Arabs and the West because, despite the history of Kurdish suffering and cultural distinctiveness, their claim to self-determination has
never been recognized, yet, the Palestinian claims to nationhood re-
ceives sympathetic hearing from the Arabs and the West.

Throughout the pre-war period and into the war period the double-
standard theme persists. In the February 3, 1991 editorial ("Dictates of
war"), the *Post* raises another issue of double standard against Israel. It
reminds the reader that Israel was criticized for restricting the press and
dismissing Arab workers during the Intifada, but during wartime, the
dismissal of Arab workers in European airports, is accepted, and, the restrictions imposed by the U.S. military on the press are praised.

Conclusion

Analysis of actors and themes in the *Jerusalem Post's* editorials pertaining to the Persian Gulf crisis and war revealed a variety of overlapping themes. The narrative that developed through the actors and
themes isolated Israel from, not only, its Middle East neighbors, but, the
international community. Major actors included Saddam Hussein, Israel, the PLO, Jordan, Syria, and Saudi Arabia. Other major actors included The United States and President Bush, the Soviet Union and
Mikhael Gorbachev, the many members of the international community
with the United Nations and the U.N. Secretary-General Javier Perez de
Cuellar.

Some macro themes, such as, the-world-against-Israel, Israel-misunderstood, Saddam Hussein-as-aggressor/Hitler, and the friends-and-ene-
mies of Israel, were developed by the editorials of the *Post*. There were
some micro themes as well. Analysis of the Saddam-as-Hitler theme
reveals that Saddam's role as villain is supported through historical references to the developments in the 1930s in Germany.

Although actors and themes are numerous and overlapping in the
text, their roles within the narrative are well defined. Israel, as well as
Kuwait, is the victim. Saddam Hussein, the PLO, and the Arab Nation
become the villains, with the international community waxing and wan-
ing in their support of these aggressors. The United States, while con-

stantly receiving criticism for its actions and non-actions concerning the PLO, is the enforcer.

Macro and Micro Themes

Saddam-as-Hitler/aggressor
   Remember-the-1930s
   Democracies-versus-totalitarian dictatorship
   Arm-democracies-only
The-world-against-Israel
   Israel-misunderstood
   PLO-terrorists
   PLO-against-Palestinians
Friends-and-enemies-of-Israel
   Bad-Arabs (Syria, Jordan, Saudi Arabia)
   Good-Arabs
   Temple-Mount-justified
   No-linkage
   No-international-conference
   Territory-gained-in-defense
   Territory-gained-through-aggression
   Where's-the-money-for-restraint
   Arab-unity-threatened
   Withdraw-and-prevent
Coalition-lineup
United States-as-enforcer
Double-standard

The Kayhan International *(Iran)*

Analysis of 114 editorials, 79 pre-war and 35 for the war period, reveal several major themes with minor themes supporting major ones. Actors are characterized within each theme as aggressors, peacemakers, controllers, and compliance participants.

The United States is the major actor from the *Kayhan International's* point of view, with other national actors including, Kuwait, Iraq, the Soviet Union, Egypt, Jordan, and Saudi Arabia serving minor roles which only comply with the U.S. policies and intentions. Iran maintains the role of an analyst and a potential peacemaker/mediator, while

Israel becomes a major actor through its aggression against the Palestinians.

Invasion-And-U.S.-As-Aggressor Themes

A discussion is best presented by approaching each major theme through minor themes supporting various roles of major actors. The invasion and the-U.S.-as-aggressor theme is supported by a number of micro themes. Through the following micro themes, i.e., the double-standard, the U.S.-vital-interest (oil), Arabs-as-victims, Sheikhs-as-pawns-of-war, Israel-threatened, Israel-as-U.S.-ally, and Bush-as-a-desperate-individual, the newspaper told the story of United States interventionism and the roles various nations played that enabled the United States to start a war against Iraq.

The U.S.-aggression theme begins on August 3, 1990 in the editorial "In search of a Tonkin Incident" and continues throughout the pre-war and war periods, when the invasion of Kuwait by Iraq occurs and the United States, according to the editorials, views this as an opportunity for it to "police" the Persian Gulf. The U.S.-vital-interest (oil) theme was established the day after Iraq's invasion of Kuwait (in the August 3, 1990 editorial) when the United States was accused of creating an international incident out of the Iraqi invasion of Kuwait that could be compared to the contrived "Tonkin Bay incident" which gave the U.S. President Johnson an excuse to announce bombing North Viet Nam. In this early editorial, Kuwait, along with Saudi Arabia and the Emirates, were described as American protectorates that were being used by President Bush to help a struggling U.S. military-industrial complex and, thereby, solve his domestic economic problems.

The Arab Nation, with the sheikhdoms of Saudi Arabia and Kuwait, are believed to be doomed from the beginning as they yielded to the United States in its demands for oil and, therefore, became victims through their own greed. On August 25, 1990, the newspaper accused Iraq of invading Kuwait because Kuwait had violated agreements on oil prices. The newspaper also accused the United States of manipulating Saudi Arabia into allowing foreign (U.S.) troops on Arab soil to protect its "Arab" oil (in an editorial, "Fighting temptation"). These intertwined themes of villain and victim continue throughout the seven-month period with the United States referred to as the primary villain in the crisis.

The U.S.-as-aggressor theme is developed through various minor themes that discuss the United States as a hypocrite. Emphasis is placed on the U.S. invasions of Panama, Grenada, and Libya, and U.S. support of Iraq's invasion of Iran (August 3,1990 "In search of a Tonkin incident," August 9, 1990 "Iraq's invasion of Kuwait from different perspectives," & August 18,1990 "Hostages to American domestic politics"). As early as August 9, 1990, the *Kayhan International* puts Iraq's invasion of Kuwait in the same category as the Soviet invasions of Czechoslovakia and Afghanistan, and, Israel's invasion of Lebanon. This early editorial points out Israel as a major actor in the double-standard theme. Israel is seen as benefiting most from the Gulf Crisis when Arab unity suffers a blow thereby allowing Israel a free hand to continue its war against the Palestinians.

In November, the *Kayhan International* pointed out that Israel and the United States were aware of Saddam's plans to invade Kuwait. It also predicted that Iraq would not invade Saudi Arabia. These statements attribute a conspiratorial liaison to the two nations where Israel would be free to attack Palestinians while the United States would establish its hegemony in the post-cold war era.

The double-standard theme continues in October when the *Kayhan International* discusses Washington's interest in solving the crisis. Where was U.S. outrage, asks the newspaper, when Iraq bullied Iran or when the Palestinians were labeled terrorists and butchered while Israel acted in the "defense of legal rights?"

The double-standard theme continued in November when the *Kayhan International* condemned Iraq's invasion of Kuwait pointing out that evidence of the alleged atrocities in Kuwait by Iraq simply did not exist, yet, these allegations were being used by Bush and Thatcher to justify force (November 14, 1990 editorial titled "Iraq worse than Israel?"). Again, the reader is reminded that the United States has not condemned the atrocities perpetrated upon the Palestinians by Israel.

The *Kayhan International* takes a stand on "linkage", a tactic used by Saddam to link his invasion of Kuwait to the Israeli/Palestinian issue, as an insincere and far-fetched excuse for his own invasion. At the same time, the editorials, while denying linkage, point to the double-standard by associating the United States and Israel as valued allies whose interests lie in controlling Muslim nations in the Middle East.

Major actors in the aggression theme were given certain attributes. While little was said about President Saddam Hussein, other than being called a bully, and an expansionist individual who was insincere to the Arab cause, President Bush was called a desperate and an aggressive individual. In an editorial ("The Kuwaiti crisis and our national security," August 8, 1990) the *Kayhan International* views Saddam Hussein not only as a ruthless leader, but as a victim, who has not only been created, but used by the United States to control oil in the Middle East.

Beginning in August, Mr. Bush is described as facing economic trouble at home including threats by the European common market and Japan (August 3, 1990 in the editorial entitled "In search of a Tonkin incident"). The U.S. military-industrial complex is seen as struggling while unemployment, race relations, education, and the deficit add to Bush's problems. The solution to some of these problems, according to the editorial, was linked with the Middle East and its oil, which explained Bush's interest in Kuwait and his desire to police the Middle East.

George Bush is described as hypocritical (the double-standard theme) while Iraq is considered reprehensible. Iraq is seen as "propped up" by the United States to invade Kuwait while President Bush uses Kuwait and the control of oil to "score domestically." Bush is described as and deluded, in his primary aim, the destabilization of the Middle East, giving him control over oil prices and a way to fix his domestic ills (August 18, 1990, in "Hostage to American domestic policy").

Bush's offer to negotiate with Saddam Hussein through Baker on January, 9, six days before the deadline set for Iraq to withdraw from Kuwait, is seen as "Reagan speak" whereby Bush has no intention of negotiating but is stalling for time to get his troops ready. Bush is depicted by the newspaper as a man who has extended a false promise to serve his own agenda. After the suggestion that solid conventional wisdom will prove to be nonsensical if the United States attacks Iraq, the *Kayhan International* predicts that if Saddam Hussein is the president of Iraq in 1993, George Bush will not be the president of the United States (December 12, 1990, in "War or Peace?").

The Compliance Theme

Analysis revealed that three micro themes contributed to the compliance theme. Through the micro themes, namely, the sheikhs-as-pawns-of-war, Arabs-as-victims, and the world-sells out to the-U.S., various national actors are depicted as weak and engulfed in self interest.

Egypt and Turkey are called harlots to the U.S. cause, Turkey for allowing U.S. bombing planes to leave its country and shutting off pipelines from Iraq, and Egypt for its part in the war in exchange for a write-off on arms payments. Within the compliance theme, the *Kayhan International* describes Jordan, Cairo, Moscow, and the Emirates as flexible allies which yield to the United States early, without much resistance to its aggressive policy.

Saudi Arabia is especially attacked as being a greedy pawn of the United States. Disparaging comments about the monarchy and the ruling families of Saudi Arabia and Kuwait bolster the sheikhs-as-pawns-of-war theme. Beginning with the first editorial after the invasion of Kuwait by Iraq, Saudi Arabia and Kuwait are seen as U.S. protectorates. U.S. backed sheikhs of pro-Western regimes (Kuwaiti and Saudi) are said to be the first to go after the United States comes into the region. The newspaper says that Kuwait has the least political and social freedoms, while the Saudi government prevents political freedom by pretending that it is protecting an Islamic system (September 11, 1990, in "First victims").

On September 18, 1990, the *Kayhan International* warns the Al-Saud dynasty (Saudi) that benefits of American intervention to the monarchy are an illusion. The Kuwaiti Al-Sabah family is called a pawn of Washington. Oil is the commodity through which the sheikhs sell themselves out to the United States. Fahd (Saudi Arabia) and Jaber (Kuwait) are told to "Feed their Guest (U.S.)" now that they have invited them onto their soil. On December 12, 1990, the Saudi King is said to be ready to send American children (troops) to their graves to protect his throne. The sheikhs-as-pawns-of-war continues as a minor theme throughout the time period until the final days of the war when oil and the sheikhs are again linked as the reason for the war. In a call to end the bombing of Iraq on February 27, 1991, the Saudi monarchy is said to have an unholy alliance with the Great Satan that has allowed Bush to destroy Iraq and destabalize the Middle East.

Iran-As-Peacemaker-And-Mediator

Two other themes involve major actors in the war. The first, the Iran-as-peacemaker-and-mediator theme, is based upon Iran's experience in solving post-war problems such as the POW exchange. Immigration and refugees are also of concern to the *Kayhan International* with the Kurds making up a very large group of people who have sought and found refuge in Iran.

The second, is the withdraw-and-prevent theme, begins a few weeks before the allied bombing of Iraq and Iraqi targets in Kuwait represents advice given by Iran to Iraq. Beginning in August, the *Kayhan International* becomes extremely skeptical of Iraq. Based on experiences from the recent and long Iran-Iraq war, Iraq is seen as territorially aggressive and, therefore, a possible threat to Iran. Early in the time period, the *Kayhan International* joins the World in demanding that Iraq unconditionally withdraw from Kuwait (August 8, 1990, in "The Kuwait crisis and our national security"). A strong stand is taken at this time because Iraq had stalled in its reconciliation with Iran over the Iran-Iraq war. However, by September, the *Kayhan International* sees Iraq as more reconciliatory in wanting a "lasting peace" between Iraq and Iran (September 13, 1990, in "Iran-Iraq ties must benefit region's peace and people"). Although the newspaper still condemned Iraq's invasion of Kuwait, food is offered to Iraq as a gesture of a "Muslim" solution. Later, Iran was said to join Iraq in fighting U.S. imperialism by confronting U.S. troops in Saudi Arabia (September 15, 1990, in "Understanding Tehran's attitude"). Equally important is Iran's position as a peacemaker within the context of supporting Iraq which further links Iran with Iraq in challenging the U.S. policy of containing Islam in the region (October 24, 1990, in "The cancerous tumor").

Although Iran's position remains unchanged on the question of the need for Iraqi withdrawal, the *Kayhan International* continued to hold Israel and the sheikhdoms responsible for the war by playing into U.S. hands. Therefore, Kuwait and the Al-Sabah family are described as ruthless suppressors of Muslims and democracy (December 10, 1990, in "Closing the Al-Sabah chapter"). The Jabers are said to have paid for the misery that Iraq inflicted on Iran during the Iran-Iraq War. Iran, according to the newspaper, did not call for Iraq's withdrawal from Kuwait and the restoration of the Al-Sabah monarchy, but, called for unconditional withdrawal and then elections.

By January, the theme changes to withdraw-and-prevent-war (January 1, 1990, in "The idea of war") that, according to the *Kayhan International*, would only benefit Israel if Iraq was broken into pieces (January 19, 1991, in "Bits and pieces"). By the sixth day into the bombing, although Saddam is declared the symbolic winner because he has sent missiles to Israel and invaded Kuwait, he is asked by the *Kay-*

han International to withdraw to stop the bombing and prevent Iraq's destruction (January 23, 1991, in "Futility of war").

Iraq-As-Peacemaker

The Iraq-as-victim and the Iraq-as-peacemaker theme took Iraq out of the role of aggressor after the bombing began in January. Throughout February to the end of the bombing and short ground offensive, the newspaper demanded that the bombing be stopped. Thus, the United States was seen as the primary enemy because it was dropping tons of bombs on innocent Muslim women and children, in thousands of sorties over Kuwait and Iraq.

While the first two weeks of the month of February emphasized Iraq as a victim of U.S. aggression, Baghdad soon assumed the role of a peacemaker when it lay down three conditions for its withdrawal from Kuwait. Iraq would withdraw, if (1.) foreign troops would get out of the region, (2.) Zionists would get out of Palestine, and (3.) Syrian troops would get out of Lebanon. While these conditions brought a strong "no linkage" statement from President Bush, the *Kayhan International* editorialized the application of a double standard again in the region, and pointed to the determination of the United States to destroy Iraq for the primary purpose of aiding its ally Israel and controlling Middle East oil (February 17, 1991, "Linkage in Persian Gulf crisis"). The February, 23, 1991 editorial, "Why war now," portrayed Saddam Hussein as the peacemaker for accepting the eight-point-peace plan proposed by the Soviet Union which included an international conference addressing the Israeli-Palestinian issue. Iraq is said to be "destroyed" because it stood up to U.S. aggression and did not heed Iran's advice of withdraw and prevent its destruction (February 25, 1991, in "Unnecessary ground assault").

Conclusion

Analysis of actors and themes in the *Kayhan International's* editorials pertaining to the Persian Gulf crisis and war revealed a rich texture that provided a very logical narrative in the context of their perceptions of the geopolitical realities. Major actors included nation states, such as the United States, Iran, Iraq, Kuwait, Saudi Arabia, and Israel. Organizational actors were represented by the PLO and the United Nations. While, leaders of nations and organizations, such as, George Bush, Saddam Hussein, Secretary General Cuellar, and the various sheikhs. Minor actors were discussed and placed within the context of supporting roles. These minor actors include countries such as, the Emirates, the Soviet Union, Germany, Egypt, Jordan, Turkey, Japan, Britain and individuals such as, Margaret Thatcher.

The narrative that was developed through the actors and themes in the editorials was based on the invasion theme. Iraq is seen as the aggressive invader of Kuwait, but it was possible only because of the U.S. policy of backing Iraq in its invasion of Iran. The editorials also point to the U.S. policy of invading Arab soil in order to control oil in the Middle East. Saddam Hussein is said to be a dictator, but, the *Kayhan International* is careful to attribute his military strength to the United States. The irony of this situation should not be lost on those who provided various forms of support to Iraq in its long war with Iran.

The sheikhdoms are victims of their own greed, and, the U.S. policy of controlling oil in the Middle East. The Arab Nation becomes a victim not only because of the loss of autonomy and freedom, but, also, because the world attention is diverted from the primary cause of conflict and injustice, the Israeli-Palestinian problem. Israel is seen as an aggressor which, with the aid of its ally, the United States, takes advantage of the Gulf crisis to discredit the Intifada in the eyes of the world.

America-as-aggressor, America-as-hypocrite (the double-standard theme) and the U.S.-vital-interests (oil) themes dominate the time periods. The United States is seen as relentless as President Bush is characterized as a desperate individual who will do anything to mend his domestic problems at the expense of Middle East peace.

At the same time Iran emerges as the peacemaker because of its experience with problems in its long war with Iraq, territorial disputes, and refugee problems. The-Iran-as-peacemaker theme unfolds as the United Nations is given responsibility to negotiate a peaceful solution to the crisis. A multitude of countries, and where they stand in reference to the peace issue, is discussed through the compliance theme with constant reference to whether their economic situations would force them to be bought out by the United States. The royal families of Saudi Arabia and Kuwait as pawns-of-war is a theme that persists throughout the period.

Equally important is the fact that no Iranian leader individually emerges as a major actor. The Iranian position of neutrality in the crisis is carefully maintained through references to Tehran reasoning from a broader Islamic perspective rather than a narrow nationalistic one.

Macro and Micro Themes

Invasion theme
U.S.-as-aggressor
   America-as-hypocrite (double-standard)
   U.S.-vital-interest (oil)
   Bush-as-a-desperate-individual
Iraq-as-aggressor
   Iraq-as-victim
   Iraq-as-peacemaker
Compliance theme
   Sheiks-as-pawns-of-war
   Arabs-as-victims
   World-sells-out-to-U.S.
Israel-as-aggressor
   Israeli-Palestinian-issue-threatened
   Israel-as-U.S.-ally
Iran-as-peacemaker-as-mediator
   Withdraw-and-prevent

Summary of Major Actors and Themes

Analysis of the editorials in six Middle East newspapers during the Persian Gulf crisis and war revealed, similarities and differences in major actors and their roles in the war narrative, and also, in macro and micro themes. Comparative analysis was approached from the Arab-nonArab perspective, but, found further groupings or clusters within the Arab newspapers. The following tables and discussion of each table will illustrate these clusters in relation to roles major actors play in the editorials, and in relation to themes, in the six newspapers.

TABLE 3.1

The role actors play in editorials in six Middle Eastern newspapers.

	Arab Nation	Iraq (Saddam Hussein)	United Nations (Perez de Cuellar)	United States (George Bush)	Israel
Arab					
Jordan Times	peacemaker	peacemaker	peacemaker	aggressor	benefits, aggressor
Syria Times	victim, peacemaker	aggressor		aggressor, interventionist	benefits
Arab News	victim	villain	peacemaker	defender	benefits
Emirate News	victim	aggressor, villain	peacemaker	enforcer	benefits
Non Arab					
Kayhan International	victim	aggressor	peacemaker	aggressor	aggressor
Jerusalem Post	villain	villain	friends and enemies	defender	victim

Roles played by major actors are divided in Table 3.1 according to each newspaper's Arab or nonArab status. This division showed expected differences in the *Jerusalem Post's* editorials where Israel takes the role of victim rather than the aggressor or beneficiary as Israel is portrayed by the other five newspapers. Israel is seen by the *Jerusalem Post* as being victimized by its long-time enemy, the Palestinians with the backing of the Arab Nation as a whole. Hence, the Persian Gulf War and the roles of the major actors in the war narrative become part of a greater narrative, that of the Israeli-Palestinian problem and where the world community members fit in relation to defending Israel from the villainous Arabs whether they be Saddam Hussein, the PLO, or collectively, the Arab Nation.

At the same time, the other nonArab Iranian newspaper, the *Kayhan International,* bases the roles of the major actors around the United States, as the primary threat to the region. Through this perspective Saddam Hussein is similarly seen as the aggressor who has violated Arab unity as a result of the United States setting up Iraq, both militarily and situationally, to transgress upon its neighbor, Kuwait. Kuwait, not shown in this chart, is depicted as deserving whatever Saddam Hussein could do to it to punish for its part in supporting Iraq during the Iran-Iraq War.

Arab newspapers can be grouped into two sections, the *Jordan Times* and the *Syria Times* which considered the United States as the aggressor or interventionist, and the *Arab News* along with the *Emirate News* which viewed the U.S. role as the defender and enforcer of Arab solidarity and a world consensus. The role of the United States as aggressor and interventionist in the *Jordan Times* and the *Syria Times* is directly related to its perceived relationship to Israel as an ally. The *Jordan Times* comes perhaps the closest to the majority Arab solution to an Arab problem. Saddam Hussein is seen by the *Jordan Times* as no more than a wayward Arab who is trying to solve Arab problems. The *Syria Times* links the United States to Israel accusing the United States of interventionist policy. It is apparent that the *Syria Times'* primary interest in forcing Iraq out of Kuwait is to get foreign troops (U.S. as interventionist) off Arab soil and to get Arab and world attention back to the Intifada.

The second set of Arab newspapers represented in the study are made up of the *Arab News* (Saudi Arabia) and the *Emirate News* (United Arab Emirates). Both newspapers gave the major actors almost identical roles in the war narrative. The United States is expected to defend Arabs and enforce a world consensus against Saddam Hussein. Saddam is demonized by the newspapers and his invasion of Kuwait is seen by them as a blow to the Arab Nation in general, and sheikhdoms in particular.

Analysis of the editorials identified specific clusters of themes. Table 3.2. identifies two Arab newspapers, the *Jordan Times* and the *Syria Times* as having two macro themes,

Arab-unity and Arabs-divided. It is interesting to note the various micro themes that are associated with these two themes in each newspaper. While the *Syria Times* does not share the *Jordan Times'* penchant for making Saddam Hussein the defender of Arab unity, it does continue to seek a peaceful solution to what both newspapers consider an Arab problem.

TABLE 3.2

Macro and micro themes in editorials in the *Jordan Times* and the *Syria Times* during the Persian Gulf Crisis and War.

Macro Themes	*Jordan Times* (Jordan)	*Syria Times* (Syria)
	Micro Themes	
Arab-unity	Arabs-as-peacemaker King Hussein-as-peacemaker Saddam Hussein-as-peacemaker Saddam Hussein-as-strong-Arab Saddam-defends-Arabs-against-Israel Saddam-gestures-to-Israel U.N.-responsibility Linkage	Assad-and-Syria peacemakers Arab-solution Withdraw-and-restore
Arabs-divided	Jordan-as-victim Saudi Arabia-as-victim Israel-benefits U.S.-drives-wedge Double-standard Foreign troops-on-Arab-soil U.S.-as-aggressor U.S.-equals-Israel U.S.-allies-behind aggression U.S.-oil-conspiracy	Iraq-hurts-Arab-cause Israel-takes-advantage U.S.-as-Israel's-ally Double-standard U.S.-as-interventionist Foreign-troops-on Arab-soil Intifada-interrupted Zionist-threat-to-Arabs

Undoubtedly, the reason for each newspaper's stand for an Arab solution to the crisis may be explained by their concern for the consequences of division within the Arab Nation. In both newspapers, the United States is seen as the aggressor along with Israel's ally. There are some common micro themes that revolve around the concern that Syria and Jordan have regarding the American interventionist policy that does not allow the Arabs to solve their own problems. Other themes involve foreign-troops-on-Arab-soil, the double-standard, the U.S.-as-Israel's-ally, and the Israel-benefits, etc.

The second set of Arab newspapers, the *Arab News* and the *Emirate News,* focused on three macro themes, Arab-unity, world-unity-and-responsibility, and Saddam Hussein-as-aggressor/Hitler. Table 3.3 illustrates the three macro themes.

TABLE 3.3

Macro and micro themes in editorials in the *Arab News* and the *Emirate News* during the Persian Gulf Crisis and War.

Macro Themes	*Arab News* (Saudia Arabia)	*Emirates News* (United Arab Emirates)
	Micro Themes	
Arab-unity	Arabs-divided Kuwait-as-victim Saudi Arabia-as-potential-victim Withdraw-and-restore No-linkage Israel-benefits	Zayed-as-wise-leader No-linkage Arab-solution-peaceful Israel-benefits
World-unity-and-responsibility	World-responsibility Foreign-troops-defend-Arab-soil U.S.-defends-Arabs Peace-through-force Palestine-and-Kuwait-are-World-issues Withdraw-and-restore	Multi-national-force-protects Bush-as-enforcer U.S.=World=U.N. Unconditional-withdraw-and-restore
Saddam Hussein-as-aggressor/Hitler	Remember-the-1930 Saddam-as-bad-Arab Saddam-responsible Saddam-equal-Israel	Saddam-responsible Kuwait-as-victim Arab Nation-as-victim Hostage

Analysis reveals that both macro and micro themes are fairly similar in these two newspapers. It becomes apparent that both the *Arab News* and the *Emirate News* quickly turn the solution of the crisis over to the world community represented by the United Nations. Implicit in this view is the U.S.-as-defender-enforcer theme which is contained in both newspapers.

Consequently, the *Arab News* and the *Emirate News* progress through a line of reasoning which recognizes Saddam's invasion as a transgression of one Arab upon another and, therefore, an Arab problem. But, since Saddam Hussein is following directly in the footsteps of Hitler and other aggressive dictators of the 1930s, the crisis has become much bigger and far reaching than the Arab Nation could and should handle. By demonizing Saddam Hussein both newspapers were able to justify foreign troops on Arab soil, and the peace-through-force strategy.

It must be remembered that both Saudi Arabia and the United Arab Emirates resemble Kuwait in many ways. Themes in both newspapers, and especially in the *Arab News,* show empathy for the Kuwaiti monarchy and defend Kuwait as an Arab nation that has been aggressed upon by an Arab brother. Furthermore, this aggression is committed by a greedy, aggressive, Hitler-type Arab who has gone power mad. Consequently, Saddam Hussein must be stopped at any cost under the guidance of the United Nations with the United States acting as the strong arm among the players.

In an inter-Arab context it is interesting to note that although Israel played a major role in the narrative of the *Jordan Times* and the *Syria Times,* it does not assume a similar role in the *Arab News* and the *Emirate News.* Unlike the other Arab newspapers, the alliance between the United States and Israel is underplayed by both the *Arab News* and *Emirate News.* However, the *Arab News* does discuss the aggressive policies of Israel against the Arabs and in an interesting twist equates Israel with Iraq for its aggression. In its support of the non-linkage policy of the allies, it is opposed to linking the Iraqi invasion to Israeli aggression on the Palestinians.

Analysis of the two non-Arab newspapers used in the study shows little similarities in macro and micro themes. Although each newspaper, the *Kayhan International* and the *Jerusalem Post,* is non-Arab, they have little else in common. Table 3.4 illustrated macro and micro themes in these newspapers.

TABLE 3.4

Macro and micro themes in editorials in the *Kayhan International* and the *Jerusalem Post* during the Persian Gulf Crisis and War.

Kayhan International (Iran)		*Jerusalem Post* (Israel)	
Macro	**Micro**	**Macro**	**Micro**
Invasion-and-U.S.-as-aggressor	America-as-hypocrite Double-standard U.S.-vital-interest (oil) Bush-as-a-desperate-individual	World-against-Israel	Israel-misunderstood PLO-against-Palestinians Bad-Arabs (Syria, Jordan, Saudi Arabia) Good Arabs Temple-Mount-justified No Linkage No-international conference Territory-gained-in-defense Territory-gained-in-aggression Where's-the-money-for-restraint Coalition-lineup United States-as-enforcer
Compliance	Sheikhs-as-pawns-of-war Arabs-as-victim World-sell-out-to-U.S.		
Iran-as-peacemaker			
Iraq-as-aggressor	Iraq-as-victim Iraq-as-peacemaker		
Israel-as-aggressor	Israeli-Palestinian-issue-threatened Israel-as-U.S.-ally	Saddam-as-Hitler/aggressor	Remember-the-1930s Democracies-versus-totalitarian-dictatorship Arm-democracies-only

Chapter IV
VALUES in the MIDDLE EAST PRESS

Editorials function as a rhetorical process whereby the newspaper discusses certain issues by explaining events based on reality judgments that are specific to the national and, thus the cultural perspective of the newspaper and the reader. Implicit in this view is the role that institutions such as religion and government play in contributing to the overall value systems of a particular national newspaper's arguments. Newspapers chosen for this study represent the national interests in the conflict zone, these newspaper editorials also embody the enduring values of their cultures.

The Jordan Times

Editorials in the *Jordan Times* for the seven-month Persian Gulf crisis and war period contained a variety of explicit and implicit values. Enduring values, explicitly named in the editorials include unity, development, democracy, and modernization. Editorials discussed the Iraqi invasion of Kuwait, the Arab Nation's collective response to the invasion, and the world community's part in forcing Saddam out of Kuwait, in the context of the Arab Nation's obligation to reach and enact a peaceful solution to the problem.

Negative values such as haste, procrastination, selfishness, and temporary or emotional interests imply that the Arab Nation must approach the problem of Saddam's invasion of Kuwait from a broad perspective. Thus, by centering the discussion around various actors, both Arab and international, and the role each plays in contributing to a peaceful Arab solution to the problem, the *Jordan Times* evaluates Saddam Hussein, the United States, Jordan, Israel, the Soviet Union, Morocco, Algeria, Saudi Arabia, and other countries in reference to two value clusters:Arab unity and economic values. Formalistic values are discussed as a third value cluster.

Arab Unity

Arab unity is discussed in the editorials by challenging various members of the Arab League to respond to Saddam Hussein's invasion of Kuwait from an inter-Arab perspective. Consequently, the United States is seen as an interventionist nation which has, not only, aggravated the situation by bringing foreign troops into the region, but, also, wants war to gain control of oil in the Middle East. Arab unity is, therefore, under threat from the outside interventionist policies of the United States which is also an Israeli ally. Consequently, the *Times* describes the United States in negative terms, such as, narrow, aggressive, and selfish. Underlying the discussion in the editorials is a constant call to Arabs to solve their own problems within the Arab Nation. Accordingly, the *Times* promotes a logical discussion from a perspective that tries to empower Arabs to negotiate a peaceful solution. Therefore, equality, dignity, unity, development, democracy, and modernization are discussed as appropriate goals of the Arab Nation.

In this context, the *Times* refers to Saddam Hussein from an inter-Arab perspective as a reasonable leader, who is not a "Hitler" as the United States is labeling him, but, who is acting within regional economic and political pressures. President Saddam Hussein, thus, becomes the defender of Arabs who wish to solve their own problems within an Arab context without interference from selfish interventionist policies of the U.S. government.

A rational discussion is presented early in August that appeals to Arabs to consider Saddam Hussein from a historical Arab perspective, while the United States is discussed as willing to sacrifice Arabs for its oil interests and in defending Israel. On August 4, 1990 in an editorial titled "Feverish campaigns and hidden facts," the *Times* discusses the political climate that led up to Iraq invading Kuwait. Saddam's speech on July 14, 1990 to the Arab League is pointed out as a warning to Arabs that Iraq's difficulties with Kuwait were increasing. Iraq, seen through the inter-Arab perspective, is described as being hurt by Kuwaiti demands for payment of loans to Iraq that were given to Iraq during the Iran-Iraq War, and, also, increasing oil production that would lower the price of oil. In this light Kuwait was seen as an ungrateful Arab neighbor that was forcing Iraq into a desperate financial situation after it had defended Kuwait during the Iran-Iraq War.

Iraq is also portrayed as the defender of Arabs when the *Times* discusses the United States as an ally of Israel which had been creating a negative political climate by blowing up the issue of Iraq presenting a chemical and nuclear threat to Israel. This issue was put to rest as a contrived propagandist's ploy by the United States and Israel to discredit Iraq in the eyes of the world. According to the newspaper, their strategy was to draw an emotional comparison with Hitler and set up Saddam as a demonic aggressive leader who was a danger to, not only Middle East peace, but, the whole world. The United States is described as arrogant in perpetuating divisions and, therefore, in dividing the Arab world.

While the *Times* points out that U.S. interventionist policies interfere with Arab rights to control oil in the region and fight for Palestinian rights, it is also quick to point out that the self interest of various Arab nations allows members of the Arab League to fall prey to these interventionist policies. In this context, the *Times*, not only reinforces the notion of Arab solidarity and the right of the Arabs to solve their own problems, but, extends a challenge to members of the Arab Nation to eschew the values of imperialist interventionism and unite under a common Arab cause.

In the editorials, Saddam Hussein takes on the role of a reasonable Arab who has a history of defending Arab values (August 4, 1990 "Feverish campaigns and hidden facts"). Jordan also becomes a peace negotiator and interpreter of Arab values through its democratic, modern stand within the Arab Nation. Jordan's strategic location next to Iraq and Israel, and its long experience of direct involvement within the Palestinian-Israeli issue place Jordan in the role of a peacemaker in the conflict.

As U.S. troops continued to escalate in Saudi Arabia, and Saddam Hussein detained foreigners in Iraq, the Iraqi position lost further ground and the world community began to stand behind U.S. militarism. At this juncture, the *Times* began a call for a dialogue of de-escalation and reasonable accommodation. The U.S. policy of unconditional withdrawal was said to be an irrational personal crusade against the Arab world that was based on hatred, emotion, and racism. Iraq was seen as a participant that was willing to negotiate through the Soviet Union, France, and China. Jordan, while admitting that Iraq must withdraw from Kuwait, promoted an Arab solution to an Arab problem through dialogue and compromise. Accordingly, King Hussein of Jordan, represented an Arab solution to the Arab Nation as essential to regional security and sovereignty.

Economic Values

The editorials approached the problem of Saddam Hussein invading Kuwait through two major themes, Arab-unity and Arabs-divided. Actors' roles in the war narrative were balanced against whether a national leader, such as Saddam Hussein, or a nation state, such as, the United States, Kuwait, or Jordan, had contributed to Arab unity, or, conversely, created trouble among members of the Arab Nation. Analysis revealed that the *Times* appealed to the enduring values of democracy, modernization, and equality, not only through promoting Arab solidarity as the proper vehicle for solving the problem of one Arab country invading another, but, through a discussion of economic values.

Oil and its control came to represent a security issue in the editorials. From the beginning of the crisis and throughout the time period, it is apparent that the *Times* considered the control of Middle East oil the responsibility of the Arab Nation. U.S. interests in the region related to the control of oil. Saddam Hussein's invasion of Kuwait was grounded in Kuwait's rejection of Iraq's claims to oil fields and a port through which Iraq could ship oil. And finally, the *Times* discussed divisions within the Arab Nation in the framework of South which has oil, and, the North which doesn't have it. Consequently, the Saudi and Kuwaiti sheikhdoms and the United Arab Emirates were allied with the United States, while the northern oil-poor countries of Jordan and Syria continue to fight for the Palestinian cause. In this context, Saddam Hussein is not only placed in the middle of the Arab fight for the Palestinians, he is also presented as the strong Arab who deserves respect in matters of control of oil by the Kuwaitis.

It must be remembered that Iraq had recently fought a war with Iran. Kuwait, the UAE, and Saudi Arabia had backed Iraq with money from oil profits which allowed Iraq to build a strong army in the region. This Iraqi army served Kuwaiti, Saudi, and U.S. interests by fighting Iran, and, therefore, it remained in the good graces of the oil producing sheikhdoms for a time. After the war had ended and Iraq began to build up a depleted economy, Kuwait demanded that Iraq repay loans from the war.

Consequently, oil and its control was viewed by the *Times* from, not just an economic, but a political perspective in the editorials. For example, the *Times* says that the United States puts its own interests ahead of Arab interests by using a double standard whereby the United States gives money for Russian Jews to settle in Israel and, at the same time, forces a war on Arabs to assure the West of cheap oil. Implicit in this view is the importance of solidarity and security for the Arab nation to unite and solve its own problems.

From the beginning of the time period, the *Times* sees Jordan as a victim in the economic war that was being fought in the Gulf. In August, the *Times* pointed out that Jordan was being forced into going along with sanctions against Iraq by the United Nations. Jordan depended on Iraq for 90% of its oil, and substantial economic aid from Iraq and Kuwait. The fact that it saw no possibility of millions of dollars in promised aid from these two countries getting to Jordan since their assets had been frozen, placed Jordan in a vulnerable economic position among the countries of the region.

In addition, the *Times* emphasized that Jordan's call for peace through a dialogue, that would include the Palestinian issue, had brought economic punishment from the world community. Accordingly, the *Times* accuses the United States of piracy when ships are boarded outside Aqaba, Jordan's only port on the Red Sea. Jordan is denied 50-million dollars of aid because of its call for peace, while Israel, Turkey, and Egypt have been compensated for losses they have incurred by their participation in the embargo and war effort against Iraq. The *Times* therefore, calls on Arabs in general, and Saudi Arabia, in particular, to solve their own problems through a peaceful dialogue that would address the complexities of the Palestinian issues along with inter-Arab economic power issues. This call by the *Times* reflects Jordan's original role as a peacemaker among Arabs which is working toward modernization, democracy, and unity in the region.

Formalistic Values

The *Times* presented a discussion of the Persian Gulf crisis and war in its editorials that was backed with historical events in the region. The lack of hyperbole, references to God, or militaristic language used in the editorials contributed to a logical and secular discussion that was willing to analyze both economic and political issues. The editorials opened with an action or step taken by one of the major actors in the war narrative and was followed by a discussion of where the event fell in the historical context of the region. Toward this purpose the United States is considered interventionist, while Saddam Hussein is seen as an insider who understands political and economic pressures in the region.

The language used in the editorials appeals to a non-aggressive, logical approach to issues of international legitimacy, security, freedom, and dignity. Arabs, particularly Saddam Hussein, are described as misunderstood by the West, while the United States is seen as selfishly acting in its own interests. The language used represents a nonsectarian approach to a discussion that called for peace, negotiation, and dialogue as the modern, democratic way for Arabs to solve their problems.

Conclusion

Analysis of editorials in the *Jordan Times* for the seven-month long Persian Gulf crisis and War revealed a rational discussion of Arab values and a call to Arabs to solve their own problems. These problems not only included Saddam's invasion of Kuwait, but by bringing up the control of oil and the Palestinian issue, included a challenge to the Arab Nation to move toward independence and security from the interventionist United States. Jordan's strategic geographic location in relation to both Israel and Iraq, coupled with Jordan's history in trying to solve the Palestinian-Israeli issue, gave the *Times* the legitimate role of an analyst and a peacemaker.

The discussion began as, and continued to be, pro-Arab and pro-negotiation throughout the conflict. Saddam Hussein remained a good, but misguided Arab throughout the crisis. The United States and Britain represented imperialism which the *Times* regarded as the true threat to Arab unity.

The Syria Times

Analysis of editorials in the *Syria Times* for the Persian Gulf pre-war and war period from August, 1990 through February, 1991 revealed positive values such as solidarity, unity, rationality, and defense. Negative values were used in the description of any nation which challenged Arab unity and the Arab homeland. Israel accordingly appeared as the transgressor, while Iraq's invasion of Kuwait was discussed as an unwelcome diversion for Arabs whose primary responsibility was the defense of the Arab homeland against Israel.

Enduring values such as unity, heroic resistance, martyrdom, rationality, pragmatism, and maturity were implied in the newspaper's advocacy of a logical approach to protect Arab unity and the Arab homeland. Therefore, value judgments concerning the roles of Iraq, the United States, Israel, and the Arab nation can be grouped according to their contribution to, or distraction from, the ultimate goal of the Arab Nation to protect the Arab homeland from Israeli territorial aggression.

Explicit and implicit values found in the editorial discussion may, therefore, be grouped under two value clusters; Arab unity and Arab homeland. Formalistic values, a third cluster, illustrates rhetorical practices used by the *Syria Times* to reinforce values expressed in the editorials.

Arab Unity

Arab unity and Islamic solidarity as an important enduring value supported all other values expressed in the editorials for the time period. Early in the discussion the editorials stressed the Arab Nation's responsibility to solve the problem of Iraq's invasion of Kuwait. Syrian President Hafez Al-Assad took on the role of peacemaker as the editorials discussed various meetings of Arab League members early in the time period. The Cairo summit provided the first official vehicle for Al-Assad to call for Iraq's withdrawal and the restoration of the Kuwaiti government as an Arab solution to a pan-Arab problem. After a subsequent meeting in Alexandria between President Assad and Egyptian President Hosri Mubarak, the newspaper called upon Arabs to accept the responsibility of containing the Iraqi problem within an Arab solution so that the Arab nation could defend both Iraq and Kuwait against "an adventure that is pregnant with grave dangers" (August 30, 1990 in "Grave and terrifying dangers"). These "grave dangers" primarily include the build-up of foreign war ships and troops in the region which, according to the *Syria Times*, were not only threatening a fellow Arab Iraqi nation, but, were diverting the attention of the Arab Nation away from its primary enemy, Israel.

The editorials linked Islamic solidarity to Arab unity when Iraq was described as violating the Algiers Agreement of 1975. Iraq used an excuse to launch a war against a brotherly Islamic nation Iran, and, therefore, weakened the Arab fight against Israel, the true enemy of the Arab Nation. The fact that Iraq is now willing to abide by the Algiers Agreement in dealing with Iran during the crisis brings up questions in the editorial as to the validity of wasting so many Islamic lives upon an endeavor which should have been directed toward fighting Israel, the true enemy of Islam.

Positive values such as solidarity, peaceful resolution through dialogue, rationality, pragmatism, and maturity were associated with the Arab unity theme with President Al-Assad and Syria as peacemakers within an Arab solution that called for Iraq to withdraw from Kuwait and restore the Kuwaiti monarchy. It also became apparent in the editorials that the *Syria Times* considered Israel and foreign interventionism the true enemies of the Arab nation. Consequently, Iraq is discussed as a wayward Arab brother who is damaging the Arab fight against Israel by creating a situation that has drawn attention away from the Intifada and opened up the opportunity for interventionist foreign troops to come to Arab soil.

Arab Homeland

An underlying value throughout the discussion of the Persian Gulf crisis and war by the *Syria Times* was the implied value of territorial defense of the Arab homeland. Accordingly, the *Syrian Times* valued each major actor in respect to the role it played in contributing to Israel's territorial expansionist activities. Iraq's invasion of Kuwait was, therefore, seen as bad because it divided Arabs and took their attention away from the Intifada. Similarly, Israel was said to have fully taken advantage of the situation by expanding Jewish settlements into Arab homelands by accepting Russian Jews, by killing Palestinians in the Jerusalem Al-Aqsa Mosque incident, and by openly wanting Iraq's military and economy destroyed so it would no longer be part of a joint Arab front against Israel.

Through the dialogue of the editorials heroic resistance and martyrdom became the ultimate Arab value that could be obtained through resistance to Zionism and Israeli oppression. The Intifada became the
symbol for Arab vigor and bravery in actively fighting Zionist expansion. Thus, any incident or actor who interfered with the effectiveness
of the Intifada was seen in a negative context.

In addition, British imperialist control of the Middle East in this century, along with United States interventionist policies during the recent
Iraq-Iran War, further explains the value placed on territorial protection
of an Arab homeland by the *Syrian Times*.

In this context, foreign troops on Arab soil can be viewed as an evil
transgression of the Arab homeland. The fact that the troops were primarily made-up of U.S. forces, an ally of Israel's, prompted the *Syria
Times* to call for Iraq to withdraw from Kuwait and restore its legitimate
government in order to rid the region of these transgressors.

Iraq was also accused of serving the enemy of the Arab Nation, Israel, by annoying the international community with its stubborn behavior. The editorials suggest that by violating international law and
norms, and drawing the world's attention to Iraq's invasion of Kuwait,
Iraq had diverted the world's attention away from the primary Arab
value of resistance to Israeli expansion and defense of the Arab homeland. Also by refusing to agree to a peaceful Arab solution, Iraq had
given the international community a justification to again dismember
the Arab homeland.

The newspaper provided an analysis of important issue such as the
Iraqi invasion of Kuwait, the need for an Arab solution to the conflict,
and the damage to the Intifada caused by the invasion, among others.
In view of Syria's fight in Lebanon against the Zionist aggression, the
paper raised questions concerning the wisdom of allowing the Iraqi
military, a primary force in defending the Arab homeland, to be destroyed in an unnecessary war.

Interestingly, the *Syria Times* did not mention the United States in
connection with foreign troops on Arab soil, but referred to the international community through the United Nations. The United States, however, was addressed directly when an editorial asked the Americans to
"make up your mind," by asking the question:are the Americans for
right and justice or aggression? (October 28, 1990 in "Double stand-
ards, once again!"). Through the double-standard theme the newspaper
points out that although the United States has stood behind the United

Nations' demand to investigate the Jerusalem Al-Aqsa Mosque killings of Palestinians in October, it is still sending aid, Patriot missiles, F-15 fighters, 700-million dollars in military assistance, and 400-million dollars to settle Jewish immigrants, to Israel. The weapons and military aid will be used against Arabs as the new Jewish immigrants pushed their settlements further into the Arab homeland. The United States is seen as an interventionist country that is arming Israel, the true enemy of the Arabs, and is willing to destroy an Arab Nation's military demanding a strict enforcement of the U.N. resolutions on Iraq. By contrast, it notes the United States' unwillingness to force Israeli compliance on other U.N. resolutions. The newspaper expresses the Arab's right to seek justice in defending the Arab homeland against the territorial aggression of Israel or any other interventionist force.

Formalistic Values

A number of rhetorical practices were used in the editorials in the *Syria Times* during the Persian Gulf pre-war and war period. Each editorial contained a title emphasizing the urgent need to solve the problem of Iraq's invasion of Kuwait through an Arab solution. Titles such as "An urgent pan-Arab task," "The tragic situation must end," "Grave and terrifying dangers!" and "Sabre rattling and wardrums" indicated a preference for, martial language, but balanced by a call for an Arab solution to the problem.

Analysis also revealed that Israel is defined as the true enemy of the Arab Nation with Iraq's invasion of Kuwait regarded as an inter-Arab problem. Iraq is described as an Arab nation gone astray through the use of language that seems almost scolding in nature. Saddam Hussein is not individualized, but, Iraq is said to be acting foolishly to achieve erroneous ambitions. When the world community unites in its resolve to force Iraq out of Kuwait, Iraq is described as a mad nation in instituting a law of the jungle to solve an Arab problem.

Israel, on the other hand, is described as an enemy and a barbarian which resorts to butchery, massacres, and employing the settlers to commit "wide-ranging terrorist attacks." Jewish settlers are described as wild beasts seeking destruction and killing at any price, while the occupation of Kuwait by Iraq is seen as a tragic situation that has "stabbed the Intifada in the back." Thus, the Intifada becomes the symbol of Arab heroism, sacrifice, and martyrdom in fighting Zionist territorial expansionism.

Historical references to the Iraq-Iran war help setup an analogy of Iraq as the bad Arab and Muslim who had, divided Muslims whose attention should have been focused toward fighting Israeli expansionism. Through analogies, repetition, and historical references the Arab-Israeli conflict is presented as the ultimate battle against Zionism to be found by all Arabs. Therefore, Iraq became a nuisance to the Arab cause.

Foreign troops also became the symbol of the imperialistic threat that persisted throughout the editorials. Consequently, Iraq was blamed for creating an excuse for the international community to intervene in Arab affairs. Interestingly, the troops were not pointed out as mainly U.S., but were referred to as "outside troops," "foreign fleets," and "foreign warships."

The United States was, however, described as an outside nation which said one thing and did another. The *Syria Times* questioned the U.S. motives in condemning Israel for the Al-Aqsa Mosque killings, then turning around to arm Israel which would inevitably use the weapons against the Arabs.

Each editorial ended with a call to Arabs to recognize what various political moves on the part of Iraq, Israel, and the international community were doing to damage the Arab defense of its homeland. Although some historical references were given to Iraq and Israel in the discussion, most arguments used an emotional approach that appealed to Arabs to confront Zionism with valor, bravery, and steadfastness.

Some editorials were written in good form and proper English, but, many contained improper verb agreements and run-on sentences. Inconsistencies and errors throughout the time period suggest that several writers with varying degrees of English language skills contributed to the editorials, however, the message was uniform with little variation.

Conclusion

Analysis of editorials in the *Syria Times* for the seven month long pre-war and Persian Gulf War period revealed a value system that included such Arab values as brotherhood, valor, bravery, solidarity, and martyrdom. These values are emphasized directly in the context of defense of the Arab homeland. An Arab solution through dialogue to what the *Syria Times* considered an Arab problem (both Iraq and Kuwait belonged to the Arab League) was accorded great value in the editorials for several reasons. An Arab solution would unite the Arabs who had become divided over Iraq's invasion of Kuwait even though their attention should be directed to the Intifada. In addition, an Arab solution would also eliminate the need for foreign interventionist troops on Arab soil. Consequently, the defense of the Arab homeland became the primary value in the editorials. Throughout the discussion, the daily presented Syria and President Al-Assad as the defender of Arab rights and justice. Despite the crisis arising out of the Iraqi invasion of Kuwait, the primary goal of the editorials was to call the Arab and world attention back to the Intifada.

The Arab News *(Saudi Arabia)*

Values, both implicit and explicit, expressed in the editorials of the *Arab News* during the seven-month long Persian Gulf pre-war and war periods may be grouped into four clusters. The first three clusters; Arab unity, absolute monarchy, and world unity overlap as the war narrative of the newspaper evaluates roles for the major actors. The fourth cluster, labled as formalistic values, is found in the rhetorical practices of the newspaper.

Although many values in the editorials were topical in relation to the Persian Gulf crisis and war, a careful analysis revealed that many were based on enduring values which could be related to the cultural perspectives of Saudi Arabia. Saudi Arabia's history of support for Iraq during the Iran-Iraq war plus shared interests in oil production coupled with shared borders with Iraq and Kuwait created a powerful, yet unspoken backdrop, for the dialogue in the editorials.

Arab Unity

Arab solidarity, stability, security, and brotherhood expressed the value of Arab unity from the beginning of the seven-month period until the days following the short ground war. Viewing the conflict as a fratricidal war in which Iraq, an Arab brother, aggressed upon Kuwait, another Arab brother, the editorials emphasized from early August 1990, a need for an Arab solution based on justice and peaceful means. While the editorials called for a return to reason and justice at any cost, the major hope for an Arab solution came through meetings of the Gulf Cooperation Council and the League of Arab Nations, where all agreed that Saddam Hussein must withdraw from Kuwait and restore the Al-Sabah monarchy.

The value of brotherhood reflects not only a value based on tribal alliances, but, is more specifically grounded in the Muslim's desire to reach a state of Ummah or unity through community. In this context, Islamic tradition dictates laws and duties which place specific importance on inter-family relationships as the vehicle to achieve acceptance into the community of believers who will ultimately obtain union with God. Where an Arab stands in relation to the brotherhood value, therefore, becomes a measure for the *Arab News* to editorialize on who is a good Arab and who is not.

Furthermore, the fact that King Fahd is the supreme religious leader of Saudi Arabia, as well as the Head of State, further allows Islamic value to be assumed as Arab values in the editorials. Consequently, King Fahd represents both the Arab and Islamic view in the editorials as he abhors the invasion of the good Arab brother, Kuwait, by Saddam Hussein, who has become the bad Arab through his aggression upon an Arab.

Upon this backdrop the *Arab News* paints a vivid picture of good and evil in the context of Arab traditional values with Arab solidarity calling for justice in the form of withdrawal from Kuwait by Saddam Hussein and restoration of the Al-Sabah monarchy. However, Arab unity alone proves ineffective from the beginning of the crisis as various meetings of the GCC and the Cairo summit produced little in the way of persuading Saddam Hussein to withdraw from Kuwait. In addition, speedy resolutions by the United Nations Security Council, and the speedy buildup of U.S. troops in Saudi Arabia, had to be explained in the editorials.

By the middle of August and directly after the failed Cairo summit, the *Arab News* quickly placed the responsibility for solving the inter-Arab problem of one Arab brother transgressing upon another into the world arena. Saddam Hussein was labeled as an evil megalomaniac who had betrayed all Arabs, including his own people by raping, killing, and looting the people of a brotherly Arab country. It, therefore, became the responsibility of the World community to deal with this Hitler-like aggressor who possessed the capacity to use chemical and nuclear weapons that could start the next world war.

A particularly pointed appeal to Saudi Arabians to accept the world community's intervention was made in the discussion when Kuwait was equated with Palestine as a world issue. Through this equation the *Arab News* moved the important Arab territorial value associated with

Israeli occupation of Palestinian lands into the world arena. A solution to the crisis became even more important as the editorials pointed out that Israel was benefiting from Saddam Hussein's invasion by taking international attention away from the Intifada and the struggle of a brother Arab. Saddam Hussein was also held responsible for Israeli police killing a number of Muslim demonstrators in the October, 1990 Jerusalem Al-Aqsa Mosque incident.

The pressure of foreign troops, especially Western troops on the Arab holyland of Mecca and Medina, had the potential of a real moral crisis to both Arab and non-Arab Muslim believers. To Arab masses and to many non-Arab Muslims across the globe, it seemed ironic that the Saudi monarch who prided himself on being the guardian of the holiest of Muslim places, would turn to the infidel West, especially to the United States. The United States had been previously viewed by the Arab masses as the protector of Zionist Israel, and, therefore, a co-conspirator in Israel's expansionist designs on the Arab lands and oppression of the Palestinians. This Saudi policy not only presented a great moral dilemma to the Saudis and its other Arab defenders, but it also raised the question of legitimacy for the Saudi government. Obviously, the political and military developments following the Iraqi invasion traumatized many Arabs, but it also posed a challenge to fundamentalist Arabs, and Muslim values and beliefs, by bringing into question the appropriatness of the government actions. The *Arab News* needed to explain and justify these apparently contradictory government actions.

Foreign troops were, therefore, justified in the editorials as defenders of the Arab Nation and people. Saddam Hussein was equated with Hitler by analogizing Saddam Hussein's invasion of Kuwait to Hitler's aggressive acts in the 1930s. Through the Saddam-as-Hitler theme the editorials made the world community responsible for enforcing the Arab demand for Saddam to withdraw from Kuwait and restore the Al-Sabah monarchy. Thus, Saddam Hussein was seen as, not just a means to inter-Arab unity, but a threat to world peace. At the same time, the Saddam-as-Hitler theme allowed the *Arab News* to place full responsibility for causing the war and the allied bombing of Iraq and Kuwait upon Saddam Hussein, a wayward Arab turned international thug who was willing to sacrifice the Iraqi people for his own adventurism.

Absolute Monarchy

While Arab unity and Saddam Hussein's breach of brotherhood dominated the discussion in the *Arab News,* the underlying value of monarchy, i.e., the legitimacy of the Al-Sabah family and its right to rule Kuwait, ran through the editorials. Through the withdraw-and-restore theme the *Arab News* reinforced King Fahd's demand for the Al-Sabah family to be restored as the legitimate government of Kuwait.

The fact that Saudi Arabia as an absolute monarchy, with King Fahd as the supreme ruler, can be closely identified with the Kuwaiti Al-Sabah dynasty strengthened the plea of the newspaper for Iraq to withdraw from Kuwait and restore the Al-Sabah monarchy. In the discussion, Saudi Arabia associates itself as a victim of Saddam Hussein's aggression through, not only the victimization of an Arab brother, but through the victimization of a royal family.

The editorials describe Kuwait as a tiny, rich, and generous country whose population has been killed and maimed by the thousands. Kuwait is also described as an unsuspecting Arab neighbor to Iraq who had previously given Iraq 19 billion dollars to help Iraq withstand Iranian armies and win the Iran-Iraq War. In another early editorial, the call to restore the Al-Sabah family as the legitimate rulers of Kuwait is reinforced by glorifying Kuwait as a good Arab nation that raises the poor and has contributed to other countries. The people of Kuwait will triumph, according to *Arab News,* and the Al-Sabah family will be restored to power.

Examination of Kuwait as an undeserving victim appears in the editorials from the beginning of the pre-war period and continues until Saddam Hussein is established as a World threat. Implicit in this view of victimization, is a plea for defending the legitimate monarchy of Kuwait. The Saudi monarchy is associated with that of Kuwait as a potential victim, and, therefore, the world community has the responsibility for protecting Kuwait and Saudi Arabia.

World Unity

Analysis showed an underlying, but prevalent assumption that the Arab Nation should be defended by the World community in general, and the United States in particular. Although during the first two weeks, the *Arab News* called for an Arab solution to an Arab problem, this approach soon turned to one of force and defense through the United Nations and the United States.

The presence of foreign troops (U.S.) on Saudi soil had to be justified early on as defensive and temporary. Furthermore, their presence had to be seen not just in the context of defending Saudi Arabia, but, the Arab Nation as a whole. In this context, the editorials extended the notion of Arab unity to the world community as well, because a world community united against Saddam could defend international law and order that the Arab Nation could not achieve on its own.

Initially, the newspaper also urged the world community to protect its oil interests because Saddam Hussein, the greedy dictator, had already betrayed an Arab brother to create an oil monopoly in the region under his control. Clearly, they saw a convergence of interests between the oil producing Arab countries and the United States and its allies in thwarting Saddam's goal. Saddam Hussein was described as a desperate man capable of creating another holocaust by using weapons of mass destruction and it, therefore, became the world community's responsibility to "cleanse" itself of this "virus." The editorials also made the "hostages" held by Saddam Hussein a failure to humanity, implying that the world would pay if it did not intervene.

Having justified the World community's need for involvement and its responsibility in solving the problem of Saddam Hussein's invasion of Kuwait, the *Arab News* turned its attention to alliances within the world community early in the editorials. The Helsinki summit, in early September, provided the backdrop for President George Bush and President Mikhael Gorbachev to join in a "policy of hope" that could peacefully solve the problem. The British and French were reminded of past alliance mistakes made in Munich in the 1930s, while later editorials called for NATO countries to "fall in line" and send money or troops.

The United Sates with George Bush as the strong determined leader emerged in the editorials as the stalwart representative of the world community who could force a peaceful solution. The French were described as "above the crowd," Germany could not send troops, and the Italians were described as "standoffish." Nevertheless, the United Nations remained the symbol and hope for a peaceful Arab solution throughout the editorials.

Formalistic Values

Analysis revealed several rhetorical devices used in the editorials. Each editorial contained a title that emphasized the immorality of aggression. Titles such as "Moral wrong knows no boundaries," "Bullying the world," and "Philanthropy of desperation," indicates a preference for martial language. Phrases and expressions such as march toward solidarity and unity, nuclear-chemical armageddon, the noose that slowly tightens, and marching in lock-step constantly reinforced a sense of the impending conflagaration.

Arab unity and solidarity as a value cluster reinforced the right of Saudi Arabia to be defended by the international community from a demonic fellow Arab. King Fahd, President Bush, President Gorbachev, and other Arab and international leaders were referred to with their appropriate titles before their names. The Emir of Kuwait always received a proper title and in some instances was referred to as Kuwaiti Emir Sheikh Jaber Al-Ahmad Al-Sabah. Frequently, in referring to nations in the international community, only the name of the country was used. References to non-Arab members of the international community, especially the United State, were generalized further, especially when the editorials referred to foreign troops (U.S.) as international troops. This strategy allowed the newspaper to emphasize the international character of the troops arrayed against Saddam. It also allowed the newspaper to deemphasize the U.S. predominance in the military forces that were building up in Saudi Arabia. Afterall, the newspaper was quite aware of the residual suspicion and misgivings of the Arabs concerning any force structure led by the United States, which was allied with Israel and the former colonial master, Britain. Thus, mention of the United States was avoided until Saddam Hussein was established as an evil threat to the Arab Nation. Later in the editorials, President Bush emerged as a symbol of strength and wisdom who was capable of promoting a peaceful Arab solution. It is interesting to note, how, despite the fact that military forces with great destructive power and potential were mobilized by the United States and its allies, the editorials were frequently talking about a peaceful solution through the show of force. This stratgy of avoidance was apparently needed to provide reassurance to the Saudis that the vast array of forces could avoid the cataclysmic conflict the nations in the region were headed toward.

Saddam Hussein became the named villain from the very beginning. He was referred to as Saddam Hussein, the thug, the master of Baghdad, a dictator, and an outlaw. The language in describing Saddam Hussein demonized him further by making Saddam Hussein the enemy of his own people, the good Arabs of Iraq.

Historical references to actions taken by various countries in the European community during the 1930s were reserved, in the editorials, for various members which wavered in backing the U.N. resolutions with money and troops. Little historical or statistical referencing occurred when discussing the United States or Saudi Arabia.

Analogies, historical references, repetition, and associations were primarily reserved in the editorials for demonizing Saddam Hussein who had allegedly violated all Arab values. Throughout the editorials Saddam Hussein was compared to Hitler and Mussolini. The remember-the-1930s theme predominated discussions of aggression against the Arab Nation. The *Arab News* drew a dichotomy between a bad Arab nation and a good one which is threatened by the evil Saddam Hussein, who was capable of using nuclear and chemical weapons.

Saddam Hussein was also held responsible for Israeli police killing Palestinians at the Al-Aqsa Mosque in October by diverting world attention away from the Intifada and the plight of the Palestinians. Thus, the Intifada became a symbol of resistance by the Arab nation to Zionist Israel whose cause was being damaged by Saddam Hussein.

The United States was discussed in the present with President Bush as a strong leader who was capable of strengthening the resolve of the Arab Nation and the world to force Saddam Hussein to withdraw from Kuwait and restore the Al-Sabah monarchy. The editorials, therefore, omitted any discussion of the generally known interest of the Americans and their allies to participate in the conflict, namely, to protect their oil interests. They also avoided discussing the relationship between the United States and Israel, a sore su bject to the Arabs.

Conclusion

Analysis of editorials in the *Arab News* for the seven month long pre-war and Persian Gulf War period revealed a value system that included Arab values such as brotherhood, solidarity, and peaceful solutions within the Arab Nation. However, as foreign (U.S.) troops began to build-up on Saudi soil and the international community began to stand-up for the United Nations' resolutions imposed on Iraq, the editorials turned to values that would denote defense of Arab values by the international community and the United States.

In order to deal with the moral dilemma caused by the Saudi invitation to foreign forces to defend the good Arabs, Saddam Hussein was villainized on a world scale which implied that Arab values were worth defending by all right-thinking nations. Saddam Hussein was held responsible for, not only invading Kuwait, but, also, the willful destruction of his own people.

The United Arab Emirates News

The editorials in the *UAE News* consisted of two-to-five contributions from various emirates per day. During the seven-month-long Persian Gulf crisis most editorials directly discussed topics related to the crisis. Analysis of the editorials indicated that these were based primarily upon Arab and Islamic values with great emphasis placed on the importance and the involvement of the international community in the Arab call for a peaceful solution to the Iraqi invasion of Kuwait. Therefore, explicit and implicit values in the editorials for the time period may be grouped into two clusters; Arab unity and defense of Arab territory through force. A third cluster, formalistic values, describes rhetorical practices used in the editorials that identify or confirm certain values.

Arab Unity

Underlying the discussion in the *UAE News* was the call for Arabs to solve, what the newspapers considered, an Arab problem. Early in the time period, Arab-Islamic values such as brotherhood, cordiality, honor, and obligation were explicitly mentioned in the editorials. Implicit in the values was the suggestions that Iraq's invasion of Kuwait could be solved through a dialogue among reasonable Arab nations. In early August, immediately preceding the invasion, editorials went so far as to say that the Iraq/Kuwait situation would strengthen Arab solidarity and deepen fraternal links between Iraq and Kuwait. In this context, Iraq was depicted as a strong Arab shield, while Kuwait was described as a brotherly neighbor within the Arab Nation.

Early editorials stressed a united Arab nation, with Saudi Arabia and Egypt especially valued for their co-operation in solving the problem presented to the region by the invasion. While the invasion is considered a rift, a row, and a "passing summer cloud" in the first week of editorials, it becomes clear by the end of the week that the seriousness of the situation to the Arab Nation was fully understood by the *UAE News*.

At this point, Sheikh Zayed surfaced as the wise leader who would perform the duty of promoting an Arab solution to Iraq's invasion of Kuwait which had, in the newspaper's opinion, changed from nearly a rift or row to a regional crisis. In addition, it is apparent that Sheikh Zayed turns to Saudi King Fahd, early in the crisis, for protection and co-operation. Accordingly, Sheikh Zayed and King Fahd call a number of summits (Jeddah, Cairo, Arab Gulf Co-operative Council) while Sheikh Zayed meets with individual members of the Arab and world community.

On August 10, 1990, after a meeting of the GCC, the *UAE News* says that a peaceful solution to the problem will come through Arab and Islamic values of non-interference of internal affairs of other countries, sovereignty, independence, and territorial integrity. Another editorial on the same day implies that Arab territorial integrity is also suffering because the Iraqi-Kuwaiti crisis has overshadowed the Palestinian issue and the Intifada. Arab territorial integrity was also said to have suffered a setback through the partitioning of Lebanon. While Israel is implied as the enemy of the Arab nation in both the Intifada and Lebanon, the *UAE News* employed a more subtle process of separating Iraq from the Arab Nation and its values. After an initial hesitation, the daily began to describe Iraq's invasion of Kuwait as an assault upon the territorial integrity of the Arab Nation as a whole.

Underlying the hyperbole, describing Sheikh Zayed as a wise active Arab leader of the Emirates who was solving the crisis through Arab unity, was a sense of fear that seemed to propel the discussion. As the crisis ran into the third week of August, and after various Arab summits produced resolutions but no implementation, the editorials turned the discussion to the Arab values of legitimacy, law, and protection.

Furthermore the build-up of foreign troops on Saudi soil and the swift actions of the world community to act through the United Nations resolutions which had, not only imposed, but, enforced sanctions against Iraq, forced the *Emirate News* to change its plea for an inter-Arab solution. Accordingly, the defense of Arab territorial integrity, law, and legitimacy became the primary focus of the editorials.

Nevertheless the editorials continued to promote a solution of the problem through Arab goodwill and respect, but, at the same time, began to separate Saddam Hussein as the bad Arab. His credibility was questioned as he began negotiations with Iran to settle territorial and POW exchange issues that had resulted from the Iran-Iraq War. The fact that the Sheikhdoms, including the Emirates, had given considerable backing to Iraq during the Iran-Iraq War and that Iran, as a non-Arab country, allowed Iraq's negotiation with Iran to be used as a measure of a good or bad Arab lent a touch of irony to the situation.

Iraq was discussed in the editorials as an invader and territorial aggressor upon a brother Arab nation, Kuwait. Kuwait, on the other hand, was portrayed as a victim of the "bad" Arab, Iraq, which had thrown aside all Arab values and "raped" a weak neighbor. The *Emirate News* quickly associated the United Arab Emirates with Kuwait as a possible victim of Iraq's aggression and looked to international help in defending the Arab Nation against Iraqi aggression. Kuwait is described as part of the Arab family as women in the Emirates form relief groups to aid Kuwaiti families who are fleeing Iraq's aggression. The editorials also declared that young men in the Emirates were giving up their lives of comfort to join other Arab troops in the fight. At the same time, Sheikh Zayed remained the uniting force who, not only is concerned with national problems resulting from the crisis, but also, is an active wise representative of Arab values who meets with Arab, Islamic, and world leaders to bring an end to the occupation of Kuwait.

Underneath the concern for political and moral order in the region, it becomes apparent that the *Emirate News* is acting upon an underlying fear that can be expected in a country such as the Emirates. It is not surprising that the editorials would turn to Saudi Arabia as a model of the good Arab. Kuwait, Saudi Arabia, and the Emirates are sheikhdoms, are oil rich, and despite the purchase of advanced weaponry, have ineffective armies. Also the Emirates' small geographical size and its position in relation to Saudi Arabia, Kuwait, and the Persian Gulf further allowed the *Emirate News* to associate the United Arab Emirates with Kuwait as a possible victim of Iraqi aggression.

Although the editorials persisted in a call for Arab unity and a peaceful resolution to Iraq's invasion of Kuwait, the possibility of Iraq heeding the Arab nation's call for Iraq to withdraw from Kuwait and restore the Al-Sabah monarchy become more remote with each passing day. Foreign troops were continuing to build up in the area, while actions taken by the international community through United Nations' resolutions against Iraq seemed to take on a life separate from and independent of Arab involvement in the matter. Consequently, the fate of the Arab Nation was placed in a larger context after the Helsinki meeting where President Bush of the United States and President Gorbachev of the Soviet Union joined in opposing Iraq. From this point on, the newspaper clearly editorialized that Iraq's refusal to withdraw from Kuwait not only endangered Arab unity but, the world order.

Defense of Arabs Through Force

In the editorials, Sheikh Zayed continued to represent Arab values of unity, dialogue, and peace in meetings with other Arab and Islamic leaders, but, he also, began to appeal to the Arab values of law, legitimacy, and territorial integrity when explaining the international community's involvement in the issue. Thus, a peaceful solution through force had to be rationalized by the newspaper.

Toward this goal the editorials took the "hostage" situation in Iraq and made it the world's responsibility to solve. The discussion then proceeded to include Kuwait as a "hostage" and, a victim of Iraq. Iraq was not only violating moral law by killing, raping, and demoralizing the Arab people of Kuwait, but it was violating international laws and norms as well.

Saddam Hussein was demonized as a bad Arab who had failed in his responsibility to treat fellow Arabs with dignity. Similarly, the Iraqi leadership is held responsible for the continued embargo, bombing of Iraq by the allies, and the destruction of his own people. Saddam Hussein was disassociated from Arab values to the point that, after the allied bombing and ground war in February, 1991 that killed tens of thousands of Iraqi soldiers, the *Emirate News* was able to give thanks to God that the war was short and had so few casualties. Obviously, by this time, the *Emirate News'* Arab psyche had accepted the fact that Iraq had separated itself so far from Arab values by violating an Arab brother that Iraqi causalities were not counted as a loss of life.

The editorials emphasized the global public opinion that favored the use of force with the U.S. President George Bush as the enforcer of world opinion. President Bush, therefore, not only represented the world community's resolve to force Iraq to withdraw from Kuwait, but, he was also labeled as the enforcer of Arab Nation's resolve to demand Iraq's compliance to withdraw from Kuwait and restore the Al-Sabah monarchy. Interestingly, negotiation was equated with compromise and weakness. Thus, attempts to resolve the crisis through negotiation by various countries in the international community, primarily the Soviet Union and France, met with a rebuff from President Bush who demanded an unconditional withdrawal on the part of Iraq. Bush was considered more powerful with each firm stand he took, while, Iraq and other countries who were willing to negotiate a solution appeared as weak. Thus the attempts to negotiate a withdrawal from Kuwait, by both the Soviet Union and Saddam Hussein in the last week of the allied bombing of Iraq, as weak was described in the editorials as a lack of responsibility on the part of Iraq. The newspaper portrayed Iraq as weak and misguided, and, therefore, responsible for the destruction of Iraq and Kuwait by the enforcer President Bush.

Formalistic Values

Analysis revealed several rhetorical practices which contributed to the emotional appeal made in editorials over the seven-month long Persian Gulf crisis. Editorials in this English language newspaper consisted of contributions from Arabic language newspapers from five Emirates. The number of editorials varied each day.

Issues discussed in the editorials related to meetings, statements by government leaders, reports circulated by the Iraqi regime, or messages to the people from Sheikh Zayed. An emotional discussion followed in the present tense with little referencing to historical facts, statistical data, or logical reasoning. And finally, "we" was used throughout to explain what "we" hope, think, praise, call on, and defend. This consistent use of the word "we" and the large number of editorials describing the wise Sheikh Zayed's latest action toward solving the crisis, strongly suggest that the editorials functioned more effectively in rallying support for the United Arab Emirate than as a logical discussion of events.

An emotional appeal to Arab values can also be seen when any Sheikh from an Emirate discussed in the editorial is described as wise, strong, and able, who can overcome obstacles "in his wise march." Saddam Hussein is contrasted with the wise sheikh and discredited as intransigent, mad, misled, and confused. He is also referred to as devouring Kuwait, as an aggressive criminal, and as an environmental terrorist.

The United States, however, is not mentioned in the editorials except in the context of George Bush's rejection of any attempts by members of the international community or Iraq to negotiate a withdrawal. Foreign troops are referred to as "international" and "Arab," but never

American. The omission of references to the U.S. presence and, also, the control of oil suggest that, although the Emirates had taken a stand against Saddam Hussein, they were not willing to lay themselves open to ridicule from other Arab nations which firmly objected to imperialism in the region.

The United Nations, consequently, emerged in the editorials as the champion of peace through truth, law, logic, and reason. President George Bush emerged as the enforcer of the will of the world community to end the crisis.

Conclusion

Analysis of the many editorials in the *UAE News* suggest a persistent, emotional, struggle to justify the presence of foreign forces, which consisted primarily of U.S. forces on the Arab land. Toward this end Saddam Hussein had to be demonized as an Arab who had lost all senses and defiled the Arab values of peace, law, and sovereignty. When it became apparent that the Arab nation could not solve the problem of Saddam Hussein's invasion of Kuwait and that the international community (U.S.) was already on Arab soil, the Arab cause became the cause of the international community and Arab values were presented as those of the global community as well.

The Jerusalem Post

Analysis for the seven-month long Persian Gulf crisis and war revealed a set of values that could be grouped under three specific clusters. However, each of the three value clusters may be placed under the overriding value, namely, the survival of the Jewish state. The three value clusters concerned independence and self-reliance, geopolitics, and no-linkage of the Palestinian issue to the Gulf conflict. All actors, both regional and international, are valued according to the *Post's* perception of the actor's role in either attacking or defending Israel. Throughout the editorials, the *Post* continued a discussion that led to and supported the world-against-Israel and the Israel-misunderstood themes.

With the survival-of-the-Jewish state as a pervasive value undergirding each editorial, pragmatism, realism, and force may be identified as positive values. These values are directly linked with independence and self-reliance that Israel must maintain in order to validate itself as a nation in the region. In Israel's case, the Palestinians, the PLO, Syria, Jordan, and Iraq play important roles in the fragile balance of power in the region.

The balance of power depends on geopolitical values whose goal is to maintain the status quo. A sudden power move among Arabs would, therefore, change the power structure of the region's political dynamics. Oil, its control, along with petro dollars generated from the sale of oil, are essential components in understanding where the *Post* found itself in the regional dynamics of the Middle East during the Persian Gulf crisis.

Analysis also revealed that the *Post's* overriding issue, during the crisis, always came back to the Palestinian issue and the PLO. While disavowing any linkage of the Palestinian-Israeli issue to Saddam Hussein's motives for invading Kuwait, the editorials constantly justified Israel's use of force in fighting the PLO. This argument is discussed under the no-linkage value cluster.

A fourth and final value cluster, formalistic values, refer to various rhetorical practices and formal structures used in the editorials. Persuasive devices used in the editorials are also discussed under the formalistic value cluster.

Independence and Self-Reliance

Analysis of the editorials in the *Post* for the seven-month time period revealed a persistent thematic preoccupation centered on the survival of the Jewish state of Israel. In this context, independence, pragmatism, realism, and experience may be identified as positive values, while the editorials preceived tyranny, weakness, and negotiation as negative values. Since the survival of the Jewish state was perceived to be dependent on military strength and force they represented positive values in the Israeli psyche.

Saddam Hussein's invasion of Kuwait was discussed by the *Post* from August 3, 1990, the day after the invasion, until the end of allied military action, as the act of a tyrannical dictator whose primary motive for invading a brother Arab country was to take control of the Kuwaiti territory and oil in the region. It is interesting to note that the control of oil was mentioned early in the time period, but, it soon disappeared as an important theme as the *Post* began to emphasize the immorality of the dictator's actions versus the morality of the democratic government in Israel. Israel is portrayed in the editorials as a nation that understands the tyranny of dictators because, historically, it has been a victim of action directed against it by the dictatorial governments in the region. The *Post* compares Saddam Hussein with the dictators of the 1930s in the editorials and portrays Israel as a nation that is threatened, misunderstood, and blamed by the international community. It bemoans the failure of the international community to understand the Israeli imperative to deal with such tyrants from a position of strength. Accordingly, weakness demonstrated through negotiation and dialogue was seen as a negative value throughout the conflict.

Early in the editorials the United States is chastised for contributing to Saddam Hussein's army during the Iran-Iraq war. The United States is described as weak in its previous dealings with the Arabs, but, the *Post* is pleased with the United States for finally overcoming the Vietnam syndrome and being ready to lead the world community in stopping the dictator, Saddam Hussein. In this context, Israel as a self-reliant democracy, depends upon the U.S. for protection against Saddam Hussein who has "bludgeoned" Kuwait, taken hostages, and taken territory through aggression.

Geopolitical Values

The underlying posture of the editorials toward Israel's right as a democracy to use force in maintaining a Jewish state can best be understood by examining the geopolitics of the Middle East region. This geopolitical examination, of where Israel found itself in relation to the surrounding Arab nations and Iran, can be approached in terms of weapons, control of oil, and religion. Still, it is interesting to note that the term geopolitics originated as a Nazi doctrine of expansion that concentrated on the reallocation of geographic, economic, and political boundaries. Maintaining a balance of power in the region from an Israeli point of view would insure the status quo. Israel could maintain its position of defense-through-force on the issue of the occupation of Arab territory, while at the time, it could be protected from any adverse shift in a balance of power in the Arab Nation.

Consequently, Saddam Hussein was described by the *Post* as a megalomaniac dictator who was raping, killing, and bludgeoning an Arab brother in order to gain control of oil in the Middle East. Throughout the editorials, Arab nations and their leaders were associated with Saddam Hussein, who was then equated with Hitler. President Hafez Al-Assad of Syria and King Hussein of Jordan were particularly suspect due to their involvement with the Palestinian territorial issue.

The sheikhdoms are described as greedy dictatorships that used their petro dollars to buy weapons from the West and arm their wayward Arab brother, Saddam Hussein, to fight Iran. Arab unity is also devalued when the *Post* implies that an Arab solution to a regional problem is usually for Saudi Arabia to bribe the aggressor.

In drawing attention to Saddam Hussein's weapons and other weapon sales to Arab countries, the *Post* reinforced the overriding value of defense of the Jewish state by calling weapons sales to Israel "weapons for peace" on August 12, 1990. Similary, the *Post* has no problem justifying the possession of chemical and nuclear weapons by Israel because it is a democracy and, therefore, it would use them solely for defense. In the editorials, Iraq, on the other hand, along with other Arab nations, is described as an aggressive dictatorship which is capable of atrocities akin to Hitler's use of chemical gases against the Jews in the 1930s.

Arab unity becomes a negative value in the editorials. Israel is described as a self-reliant democracy which understands the value of defense and strength to protect itself in a very unstable region.

As the world community begins to form an international alliance, the *Post* continues to evaluate the various players according to whether they are willing to negotiate Saddam Hussein's withdrawal from Kuwait, or to use force in dealing with the wayward Arab. China, Italy, and the Soviet Union are thus, described as weak in the editorials, while the United States, with George Bush as its leader, surfaces as the only member of the international community which understands and is willing to use force against Iraq. Peace through force justifies actions against Israel's powerful Arab neighbor, Iraq. Nevertheless, the *Post,* in its editorials, supports the reluctant Israeli policy to restrain itself from countering Iraqi missiles during January and February of 1991.

Although the United States provided Israel with Patriot missiles and other military equipment and personnel, the *Post* continued to present Israel as the misunderstood victim of Arab aggression. However, despite the defensive help given to Israel by the United States, the editorials maintained the forceful stance that Israel should be rewarded for restraining itself from attacking Iraq. In fact, through demands for money for restraint and money for resettlement of the Russian Jews, the

Post implied that the survival of the Jewish State of Israel was the responsibility of the world community. It must also be remembered that the Saddam-equals-Hitler theme and the remember-the-1930s theme were presented consistently throughout the time period. These references to the Jewish experience with Hitler, coupled with a constant discussion of the threat of chemical attack on the Israeli population, depicted an image of a nation that was again being persecuted for being Jewish. The persecutor, in this case, was Saddam Hussein, a megalomaniac Arab who had to be stopped and destroyed so that he could not threaten Israel again.

No-Linkage

From the beginning of the crisis, and throughout the war period, the question of linkage dominated the editorials. The *Post* discussed defence, security, territorialism, pragmatism, and realism as positive values in dealing with the Palestinian issue. Yasir Arafat and the PLO were pointed out as the real enemies of Israel. They were quickly named as terrorists who, not only had no regard for the sovereignty of the State of Israel, but did not represent the good Arabs in the dispute. Therefore, it argued that since the Palestinian insurgency/Intifada had been waged and launched by the PLO, and, the PLO is a terrorist organization, there was no way for the Israelis to settle the Palestinian issue through negotiations. Defence of the Jewish State, therefore, depends on its ability and willingness to use force to solve the problem. The Palestinian issue was also considered an Israeli national issue that was to be solved within an Israeli national context.

In August, 1990 the discussion of the Palestinian territorial issue was based around the territory-gained-in-defense and the territory-gained-in-aggression themes. On August 13, 1990, in an editorial titled, "Saddam's new ploy," the *Post* makes its first disavowal of linkage of the Palestinian issue to Saddam Hussein's invasion of Kuwait. In this editorial, the Golan Heights, the West Bank, and the Gaza Strip are described as territory gained in defense. The disputed areas are considered legitimate Israeli territory because they were gained in what it considered the defensive Arab-Israeli War of 1967. Saddam Hussein's territorial gains were illegitmate, having been made through overt aggression, and, therefore, should not be compared to Israeli occupation of what the PLO and Arafat considered Arab lands.

In September, and after the Helsinki summit, where the Soviet Union brought up the need for an international conference to settle the Palestinian-Israeli issue with President Bush, the no-linkage theme predominated the editorials. The enemies-of-Israel theme developed through a lining-up of countries who were willing to "sell out" Israel by supporting an international conference. The editorials continued to point out that the PLO was a terror-motivated organization that was supporting Saddam Hussein in his aggression. Specifically, France, Italy, the Soviet Union, China, Syria, and Jordan were described as enemies of Israel, while the United States and Britain came out of the debate as the only friends of Israel.

In October 1990, the no-linkage debate took a more desperate turn. The Temple Mount "tragedy," occurred when Palestinians were killed by the Israeli Defense Forces for protesting the annual request by the Jews to lay a corner stone to a temple they wanted to build on the Al-Aqsa Mosque site in Jerusalem. The act, on both the Palestinian and Israeli sides, was filled with symbolism and could not have come at a worst time for the Israelis. In the editorials, Israel defended its right as a democracy to deal with the terrorist Palestinians who were, not only threatening the Jewish State, but, also, were taking advantage of Saddam Hussein's linkage proposal to draw international attention to their cause.

Accordingly, after Israel refused to allow a U.N. mission into Israel to investigate the killings, the friends-and-enemies-of-Israel theme got more visibility. In a clear attempt to delegitimize the Palestinian struggle and their demands for investigation of the killings, the *Post* constantly referred to the PLO as a terrorist organization. After Saddam Hussein was forced out of Kuwait, the *Post* claimed a victory for democracy over an Arab dictator and his PLO terrorist supporters with the suggestion that both got what they deserved.

Formalistic Values

Analysis revealed several rhetorical practices used in the *Jerusalem Post's* editorials. Arguments were presented in a format based on a logical and rational discussion of issues. The editorials quoted various world leaders in making their arguments, used specific numbers in their discussion of the force build-up, and referred to relevant U.N. resolutions to convey a sense of authority and history. While the discussion was presented in a rational tone without resorting to hyperbole or trying to build up an Israeli leader who could solve the problem, it is apparent that the newspaper promoted force as the only answer to the problem. Verbal attacks on the PLO, along with persistent references to the PLO as Saddam Hussein's ally, not only represents an attempt to discredit the organization, but, it also, suggests that the *Jerusalem Post* is editorializing from a defensive position. The *Post's* demonization of Saddam Hussein as Hitler adds to the sense of the experienced victim.

Conclusion

The discussion in the *Jerusalem Post* called for a pragmatic, realist, and unemotional approach to the problem of Saddam Hussein's invasion of Kuwait. Force became a positive value as a way to enforce the rights of the Jewish State of Israel to maintain its existence. The newspaper presented an image of Israel as an independent, self-reliant nation which was trying to maintain its existence in a hostile and unstable region.

The Kayhan International *(Iran)*

Editorial dialogue in the *Kayhan International* for the seven-month time period of August, 1990 through February, 1991, centered around a discussion of major actors and their roles in solving or contributing to what the *Kayhan International* considered a regional dispute. Topical values relating to the United States, Saddam Hussein, other Middle Eastern countries, the Soviet Union, and the United Nation were expressed through negative values. The *Kayhan International* regards values such as aggression, military force, interventionism, vulnerability, dependence, shallow judgement, expediency, and self-righteousness as negative and undesirable in reaching a solution to the crisis. It may be assumed that the *Kayhan International's* proposed role for Iran as a peacemaker could be effective because Iran was working from implied positive values such as honesty, tolerance, stability, solidarity, sympathy, and Islamic brotherhood.

Enduring values in the editorials can be grouped into five clusters:religious (Islamic), Middle East autonomy, economic, alliances, and formalistic. Other clusters such as the importance of family and the undesirability of war could be discussed as separate clusters but, for the purpose of this study are included in the five above-mentioned clusters.

The five value clusters will be discussed in the framework of actors and themes in the editorials. Analysis has shown that enduring values create the perspective from which the newspaper creates reality judgments and, therefore, defines the role of actors in the war narrative.

Religious Values

When taking Islamic values into account in the *Kayhan International's* editorials, it is important to remember that Iran's 1979 revolution that ousted the Shah and Rastakhiz, the Iran National Resurgence Party, was based upon a call by Ayatollah Khomeini, a Shi'ite Muslim religious leader exiled in France, for Iran to return to the principles of Islam. The ousted Shah, with the support of the United States and other Western countries, had established a one-party system in Iran. He had concluded agreements granting concessions to a consortium of eight companies, and divided large estates into small farms. As a result, he was accused of acting in opposition to traditional Islamic values. This revolutionary call gained in popular support which resulted in a constitutionally elected president in 1980 and the establishment of the Wali Faqih, a Shi'ite-clergy-appointed religious leader with supreme authority over the government. Thus Islam became the basis for all realms of private and public discourse in Iran.

Each title of the editorials in the *Kayhan International* is preceded by the statement "IN THE NAME OF THE MOST HIGH." This invocation reflects the Islamic value of forthrightness and ethicality in all matters, both individual and civil, as dependent upon the degree of religiosity possessed by the speaker, in this case the *Kayhan International*. From this and other references to Islam in the discussions, it becomes apparent how Islamic principles permeate all public and private spheres.

Islam is a religion that is driven by laws. Specific rules governing prayer, marriage, fasting, civil and private life are centered around the Ibadet (acts of devotion) and the Shari'a (the law), with these acts of devotion mandatory for membership in the Ummah or the body of believers. Because the ultimate quest in Islam is to join a community of believers combined with the application of laws governing civil matters pertaining to all actors within that community, Islamic values are important in deciding what is just and appropriate in reference to members in the community.

From this perspective, the *Kayhan International* approached Saddam Hussein's invasion of Kuwait as an inter-community problem. Even during this conflict, the newspaper quickly pointed to Israel as the aggressor because of its mistreatment of Palestinian Muslim brothers. The United States, in its view, had a history of aggression and betrayal. It had provided military assistance to Iraq during the eight-year-long conflict between Iraq and Iran. Furthermore, according to the *Times,* the U.S. policy was designed to help Iraq fight the Islamic Republic of Iran and destroy Islam as a political force. Consequently, the editorials accused the United States of trickery, betrayal of friends, interventionism, and hypocrisy—all negative values. Interestingly, it saw Saddam Hussein, despite his bloody eight-year war with Iran, not only as an aggressor, but also as a victim of U.S. interventionism and betrayal.

Islam is a religion of surrender to God's will with an individual's state of peace dependent upon his/her submission to that will. Thus, Islam, as many other religions, is concerned with humanity and the elevation of the masses through community. Individual rights are superceded by the rights of the society with relationships strictly governed in family and civil matters. Islam is also a patriarchy with rules and laws governing the duties of family members which are strictly enforced for the good of the whole.

The editorials in the *Kayhan International* were surprisingly devoid of direct references to God and religious doctrine. Most references to the Muslim world view can be seen through the value placed on family. Thus, Palestinians are called the children of Palestine who are degraded and killed by non-Muslims. The Iraq-Iran POW exchange is discussed with concern for the sons of Iraq returning from war to fight yet another bloody war. Saudi Arabia is condemned for allowing American children (soldiers) to be sacrificed in order to perpetuate its greedy monarchial control over its people. The United States is described as perpetuating the deceitful relationship of "Great White Father" and Uncle Sam in order to draw weak Arabs, particularly Kuwait and Saudi Arabia, into its plot to get an Arab brother to fight another Arab brother.

Saudi Arabia's Islamic credentials are regarded as weak, not only because its monarchy denies civil rights to the masses, but because it allows the desecration of Islamic shrines. Mecca and Medina are threatened, according to the *Kayhan International,* not only by a U.S. presence in the area, but, from a U.S. policy characterized by hypocrisy and double standard as evidenced in the "bloody suppression of the Hajj demonstrations in Mecca in 1987" (September 9, 1990, "First Victims"). Any non-Muslim influence on shrines is considered a direct assault on the Muslim believers who are working toward meeting requirements that would allow them to attain perfect unity with God.

Muslim laws strictly define the conduct of the individual creating the attitude that the good of the society overrides the right of any one individual to contribute to its disorder. This approach to human rights allowed the *Kayhan International* to see President Bush as a desperate man who could not control domestic problems of drugs, alcohol, and racism. A weak economy and the decreasing need for a strong military were said to drive Bush to disrupt the Middle East. From this perspective, the *Kayhan International* describes the U.S. citizenry not only as a self-indulgent group of individuals, but, it sees Bush as bending to this corrupt society. He is seen as a self-indulgent leader who is willing to react with a quick fix to domestic problems by causing unrest among Muslims who are governed according to rules that promote community rather than individualism.

Middle East Autonomy

An underlying posture in the discussion of the Persian Gulf crisis and war was that imperialism on the part of the British and the United States had confused issues that were strictly Middle Eastern. There are many historical references of interventionism, such as, the United States supporting Iraq during the Iran-Iraq War, the granting of Palestinian lands to Jews in 1947 by the United Nations, and the introduction of foreign troops on Middle East soil to force Saddam Hussein out of Kuwait. These interventionist policies not only interrupt the dialogue of solidarity, but create division among various nations. Thus, Saudi Arabia, Kuwait, and the United Arab Emirates are accused of being protectorates of the United States.

The *Kayhan International* stresses balance and dialogue that depends on mediation between sovereign nations. Therefore, outside interference directly discredits the wisdom of Middle East people, and implies their inability to solve their own problems through logic and common sense.

Middle East autonomy is particularly important as an underlying value in the proposed role of Iran as a peacemaker. According to the *Kayhan International*, Iran, through its revolution and recent war with

Iraq, has experienced the results of outside interventionism. Through this experience Iran has seen the value of keeping Middle East problems free from outside interference, and gained a better understanding of the value of negotiating. Iran's interest in solving the problem of the fate of the Kurds is a good example of the value placed on self-determination, goodwill, and co-operation based on experience. The *Kayhan International* also, placed Iran in the peacemaker role concerning the Kurdish issue based on Iran's experience with refugees during the Iran-Iraq war. Experience is seen as good in solving problems of autonomy along with providing security for the region. In these contexts, Iran emerged, in the editorials, as the ideal defender of Middle East autonomy.

Economic Values

Oil and its control was an underlying component throughout the entire pre-war and war periods. While the discussion continually placed the control of oil as the primary interest of the United States in its interventionism, Saudi Arabia, Kuwait, and the Emirates were also blamed for its mismanagement. Oil was described as the "lifeline" of the Middle East which could also make puppet governments out of sheikhdoms. Greedy Sheikhdoms (Kuwait) create situations that provoke invasions (Iraq in Kuwait) to solve those issues.

Oil is a relatively new commodity in the Middle East literally separating the haves from the have-nots. In addition to the basic economic value to each oil producing country in the Middle East, the control of oil remains an important political issue. While the *Kayhan International* discussed oil and its control as a problem to Middle East autonomy, it is apparent that it can be associated with other values as well.

In the editorials there is an underlying understanding that the Islamic Republic of Iran has experience in taking control of its oil production. There are constant references to OPEC and the power of inter-regional organizations to protect Middle Eastern interests. However, oil takes on a different value when the editorials approach the subject from an intra-Middle-East perspective.

The Islamic Republic of Iran, it must be remembered, enjoys a long and established reputation as the Persian empire. This history of growth in civil and cultural matters coupled with stringent Islamic laws underlies the editorial discussion of Arab countries in the region. Oil, its use and control, is used to compare the Arab nations to each other, but the editorials find the sheikhdoms as greedy and inexperienced, and, therefore, easy prey to outside interventionism. In this context, the oil and its control is used by the editorials as a contemporary measure by which to judge the worth of Arabs who had wandered the desert as nomads not so many years ago.

Alliances and Oaths

The importance of alliance and oaths in the form of resolutions, agreements, contracts and treaties is apparent in the *Kayhan International's* discussion through the seven- month period. Although the importance of alliances in territorial disputes is apparent in war narratives as a whole, certain unique qualities to this value can be found in the *Kayhan International's* discussion. References to the effectiveness of the Gulf Co-operative Council (GCC), the Arab League, and OPEC appeared to consistently provide a list of allies for and against the United States. United Nations' resolutions concerning the Iran-Iraq War, Israeli-Palestinian territorial disputes, and Iraq's withdrawal from Kuwait were discussed under the double-standard theme. And, among many other references, Iraq was given special credit for abiding by the 1975 Algiers accord in the exchange of POWs between Iraq and Iran while, at the same time a certain pride was expressed concerning the Islamic Republic of Iran "duly" observing sanctions against Iraq.

In the discussion, there are references to the corruption through trickery by George Bush and the United States when they did not abide by treaties and resolutions. Acts of trickery were described as "unmanly" suggesting the importance that the value-filled saying, a man is as good as his word, holds for the Iranians.

Although the editorials create an impression of the Iranian as a contemporary urbanite, the present society has distinctly tribal roots. Alliances and oaths as a positive value are especially important when viewed from the perspective of the tribal society. In the traditional tribal system the pastoralists gain access to much-needed territorial benefits through alliances as they move between various territories. Consequently, oaths and pledges became the law and the ultimate value became a matter of honoring alliance obligations.

In the editorials, underlying implications of the law, contractual obligations of the law, and the Islamic religion's requirements to honor the law further explain the importance of oaths in the Iranian culture.

Moral judgments can, therefore, be made from a rational, logical point of view. Hence, rationality and logic also become important values.

Formalistic Values

Analysis revealed several rhetorical practices used throughout the *Kayhan International's* editorials that can also be used to identify value systems. Arguments were presented in a discussion-type format that began with a reference to a developing issue pertaining to the war and Iran's interest in it. A logical analytical discussion followed with references to historical events, statistics involving percentages, distances in kilometers, numbers of troops, and sources referenced. The editorial ended in a one or two-paragraph opinion section in which it recommends to the players the proper and logical action to be taken to resolve the issue.

This analysis presents a logical and rational value system and implies that the reader is capable of understanding the logic expounded by the *Kayhan International.* There are no references to religion, except in discussion concerning sacred shrines in Saudi Arabia, however, a block lettered "IN THE NAME OF THE MOST HIGH" appears before each title reminding the reader of the importance, legitimacy, and the pervasiveness of the Islamic thought that follows.

Metaphor is used sparingly; however, when used it tends to suggest a certain inside savvy to the situation. For instance, when discussing the benefits of U.S. troop-buildup to the Al-Saud family, the *Kayhan International* says, "Time, however, will prove this notion as illusionary as any desert mirage" (September 19, 1990, in "The guests of Jaber and Fahd"). The Al-Sauds and Al-Sabahs are later said to "have sand in their eyes" if they think the United States will take heavy casualties to keep them on their thrones.

The proper use of familiar idioms in the English language suggests the newspaper's sophistication in translating editorials into contemporary, idiomatic English. One editorial is titled, "Wake up and smell the coffee!" while the western media are accused of "slinging mud" in another. An editorial on December 27, 1990 titled "War or peace" began with "Who knows? This desk does not claim such powers of divination and the best we can do for the moment is rehash the latest scuttlebutt." Later in the editorial the U.S. deployment of troops during the Iran-Iraq war to protect shipping in the Gulf turned out to be "Reagan-speak" for attacking Iran.

Individual leaders other than Iranian were singled out as tricky, greedy, or wriggling, but always named with his full title such as President George Bush or President Saddam Hussein, whereas references to the Iranian government were made simply and non-descriptively to Tehran. However, sheikhdoms and their leaders were named without their respective titles. This use of titling in the editorials suggests the value put on political power in relation to Iran's position as observer and mediator. Sheikhdoms were considered to be greedy, but in the context of a weak victimized power position, and, finally, the United States, Iraq, and other countries were recognized as powerful and "victimizing" and, therefore, a force to be reckoned with.

Intertextural media referencing allowed the *Kayhan International* still another formalistic device through which the newspaper gave the impression that it understood the more sophisticated underlying dynamics of power in the crisis. The Western media were singled out as responsible for creating one-sided images of Israel, Saddam Hussein, and the Middle East for the purpose of persuading the world community, while the *Kayhan International* used specific news sources such as the Associated Press, the Saudi Press Agency, newspapers in Al-Bilad and Al-Nadwa, the Israeli newspaper *Maariv,* the Jordanian daily *Al'Sha'ab,* and other Middle East news sources to validate the integrity of the "Middle East" media. When the *Kayhan International* referred to Iranian news sources it named the newspaper vaguely with phrases such as "In Tehran, one newspaper," which contributed to the image of the Iranian government as a united power that is not dependant upon individuals for its power.

Conclusion

Analysis of the editorials in the *Kayhan International* showed a sophisticated and logically developed dialogue within the framework of a war narrative which suggested the inter-relational qualities of regional, national, religious, economic, and international value systems. In addition, the rhetoric of these value systems developed through formalistic practices, not only contributed to, but reflected the value systems revealed in the discussion.

Summary of Values

Analysis of the editorials in six Middle East newspapers during the Persian Gulf crisis and War revealed value clusters that were specific to certain pairs of newspapers in the study. The obvious division of groupings is to have the Arab newspapers in one group and the non-Arab newspapers in the other. However, analysis revealed that the Arab newspapers can further be broken down into two groups: the Persian Gulf Sheikhdom newspapers, the *UAE News,* and the *Arab News,* and the northern Arab newspapers, the *Syria Times* and the *Jordan Times.*

In each of the six newspapers a hierarchy of values showing the importance of cultural anchors such as Arab unity, Islamic unity, and the right of the Jewish state to exist, illustrate how each editorializes from a cultural and inter-regional perspective. Accordingly, the Arab nations depended upon the values associated with Arab unity as their basis for discussion, while the *Kayhan International* based its discussion on Islamic values and attack Arab unity as an inappropriate way to approach the problem of Saddam Hussein invading Kuwait. The *Jerusalem Post,* similarly, attacks Arab unity, and, in doing so, offers a solution based on the right of the Jewish state of Israel to exist and assumedly use force in its defense.

The Arab News (Saudi) and the UAE News (United Arab Emirates)

Analysis revealed that the concept of Arab Unity contained a different set of hierarchial values in the Arab newspapers. Accordingly, the editorials in the Gulf sheikhdom newspapers depended on Arab unity through a hierarchy of values which was superceded by a call for solidarity, stability, security, honor, and obligation. Thus, the *UAE News* and the *Arab News* implied that the Islamic value of ummah, which deals with the social order through law thereby allowing the individual to participate in the community of Islam, is the overriding value in the Arab unity theme. The appeal to this concept is apparent through the value of brotherhood among Arabs.

In the very beginning of the crisis, both newspapers editorialized Saddam Hussein invading Kuwait as a problem that should be solved from an Arab perspective. This perspective depicted Saddam's invasion of Kuwait as a fratricidal problem that Arab sense of justice, obligation, and cordiality could solve.

However, within a short time period, the editorials had to explain the presence of U.S. troops in Saudi Arabia and the Arab Nation's inability to get Saddam Hussein to withdraw from Kuwait. At this point, the absolute monarchy becomes the value of choice in the discussion. Sheikh Zayed of the UAE, and, King Fahd of Saudi Arabia become the wise leaders who represent the people of the Emirates and the Saudis. From this perspective the newspapers appeal to the values of sovereignty, independence, and territorial integrity, while at the same time, associating the sheikhdoms of Fahd and Zayed to the ousted Al-Sabah monarchy of Kuwait. Thus, Saddam Hussein was labeled as a bad Arab who defiled, not only an Arab brother, but a sheikhdom, and, therefore, deserved to be forced out of Kuwait whatever the cost.

In establishing force as a value, basic Arab values such as peaceful solution, Arab solidarity, and cordiality, that were discussed in the early days of the crisis, were put aside. Saddam Hussein was demonized by characterizing him as a bad Arab who had raped and killed Kuwaitis. On the international level, Saddam Hussein had taken hostages, and, because he was a dictator similar to Hitler, had the potential to use chemical and nuclear weapons. Consequently, it became the responsibility of the international community to force Saddam Hussein to withdraw from Kuwait and restore the Al-Sabah monarchy. Thus, the U.S. troops in Saudi Arabia, were explained as international troops which were there to defend the Arab Nation as a whole, rather than the sheikhdoms in the region.

Interestingly, the control of oil was mentioned only briefly and in reference to Saddam Hussein. Also, while Saddam's invasion of Kuwait was said to distract attention away from the Intifada in a few references to the Arab cause involving the Palestinian-Israeli issue, references to these issues were noticeably absent in the editorials. By omitting a discussion of oil and the Palestinian issue, the *UAE News* and the *Arab News* illustrate the moral dilemma in which the two Gulf states found themselves in relation to the United States coming to the defense of the Arab Nation and the sheikhdoms. These omissions similarly suggest that the sovereignty of Arab soil, the value involved in the Palestinian territorial issue with Israel, was being violated in Saudi Arabia by the United States, which was also a recognized ally of Israel. Oil, and its control, was not discussed, which suggests that the newspapers did not want to call attention to such a volatile economic issue considering the history of U.S. interests in the Middle East region, along with the sheikhdoms' compliance in matters of oil. Therefore, both economic and geopolitical issues were omitted from the discussions and subsequently replaced with a justification for force by the international community in defending the Arab Nation's values of legitimacy, territorial integrity, and law.

In the editorials the United Nations became synonymous with the world community and represented the values of international law and norms through the values of truth, law, and logic in trying to resolve an issue that the Arab Nation could not resolve. Saddam Hussein was described as a dictator on an international level, who could only be dealt with by the international community.

Thus, force became the overriding value in solving the problem with the United States as the enforcer of the world's opinion. In fact, negotiation and compromise, values that were called for in an Arab solution, were viewed as a weakness, rather than a strength by the end of the time period.

The Jordan Times and the Syria Times

Analysis revealed that editorials in the *Jordan Times* and the *Syria Times* contained a hierarchy of values that were similar. Just as analysis had revealed similar values in the editorials of newspapers representing the Gulf sheikhdoms in the South, the newspapers from the northern part of the region produced editorial discussions which promoted similar values in solving the problem of Saddam's invasion of Kuwait.

Arab unity and solidarity was the primary value expressed in each newspaper as they discussed their basic approach to the crisis. While the solution rested within the context of an Arab solution for both newspapers, the approach varied between newspapers. It must also be remembered that both Syria and Jordan have secular governments. In fact, Iraq and Syria are controlled by the Baath party which promotes secularism in government matters. Jordan, on the other hand, is a constitutional monarchy with a bicameral National Assembly.

Similarly, both Syria and Jordan are non-oil-producing states and, therefore, do not associate themselves with the oil-rich sheikhdoms in the south. This lack of petro- dollars along with each country's adjoining borders with Israel and Iraq place each in a unique relationship with Iraq and its neighbor, Israel.

In these contexts, Arab unity plays an important role in each newspaper's approach to solving the problem of Iraq invading Kuwait. Accordingly, in the *Syria Times* Arab unity is expressed through the values of solidarity, rationality, pragmatism, and maturity. Where, in the *Jordan Times* Arab unity also has positive values such as solidarity and pragmatism, but extends Jordan's goal further to include development and modernization.

It is apparent, however, that while each newspaper seeks to contain the solution to Iraq's invasion of Kuwait within the parameters of an Arab solution, each newspaper has a specific interest in promoting Arab unity. In either case, analysis revealed that the Palestinian issue and the Intifada played an important role in each newspaper's approach to the Arabs solving, what each considered an inter-Arab problem.

The *Syria Times* discussed the invasion of Kuwait by Iraq as an afterthought in relation to the Intifada. Syria, with President Hafez al-Assad, has long been a champion of the Palestinians' fight with Israel for territory and their rights. Syria's fight against Israeli aggression in Lebanon also has a long and bitter history in the region. In this context, therefore, Iraq invading Kuwait was seen by the *Syria Times* as a nuisance which had to be solved so that the Arab Nation could return its attention to the Intifada.

Toward the ultimate Arab value of defense of the Arab homeland, the newspaper called for heroic resistance, martyrdom, rationality, and territorial defense in dealing with the Israeli transgression of Arab lands. In relation to Iraq, the *Syria Times* described it as a foolish Arab nation, which should withdraw from Kuwait under Arab guidelines proposed in a peaceful Arab solution. The *Syria Times* professed that it was the Arab Nation's responsibility to solve this inter-Arab problem in order to protect both Iraq and Kuwait from the interventionist policies of the West, to get foreign troops off Arab soil, and, to get the Arab Nation's interests back to the Intifada. Thus, the ultimate Arab value of Arabs defending the Arab homeland overrode any other reasoning in solving the problem of Iraq invading Kuwait.

The *Syria Times,* however, eventually gave in to the inevitable, and admitted that Iraq would have to be forced from Kuwait by the United Nations troops. This came as more of a resignation to the fact that the only way to get foreign troops off Arab soil and get the Arabs' interests back to the Intifada was to go along with the international community's show of force. It is interesting to note that the newspaper avoided naming Saddam Hussein, but referred to the nation of Iraq as the aggressor. Similarly, the newspaper avoided singling out the United States as the primary interventionist world power which was building up troops on Arab soil. Troops were referred to as "foreign," while the newspaper did not personalize the Iraq-Kuwait issue, but simply referred to Iraq's invasion of Kuwait. Accordingly, by referring to the Arab nation of Iraq instead of personalizing the problem to Saddam Hussein, the newspaper further implied that Iraq's invasion of Kuwait was an inter-Arab problem that involved Arab nations and should be solved in this context.

On the other hand, the *Syria Times* singled out the United States by referring to its double standard in dealing with Syria's and the Arab Nation's true enemy, Israel. By referring to specific implications of the U.S. alliance with Israel and labeling the buildup of troops in Saudi Arabia as "foreign," the newspaper suggests that the United States might become the greater threat to the Arab homeland. The defense of the Arab homeland through heroic resistance, martyrdom, rationality, and pragmatism among Arabs dominated the editorials.

The *Jordan Times*, approached Iraq's invasion of Kuwait, not only as an opportunity to solve this problem through peaceful dialogue and negotiation, but also, the ever-present Palestinian issue. But, unlike the single focus professed by the *Syria Times* for Arabs to solve the problem so that the Arab Nation could get back to fighting the Intifada, the *Jordan Times* challenged all Arabs to solve the Iraqi problem through an Arab consensus.

Toward this goal, Iraq's invasion of Kuwait was discussed by the newspaper as an economic and political inter-Arab issue. Economic values were reinforced by logical discussions of Kuwait's economic association with Iraq and the protection Iraq provided to Kuwait during the Iran-Iraq War. Kuwait's subsequent request for Iraq to pay back the loans it made during the war, plus increases in oil production, resulting in a lower price of oil, put undue pressure on Iraq which was already suffering financially. The *Jordan Times* described Iraq as a defender of Arab sovereignty where it recounted Iraq's role in the defense of Kuwait against Iran.

Oil and its control also became a security issue in the editorials. The United States was seen, by the *Jordan Times* as an interventionist nation whose only interest in forcing Iraq out of Kuwait was to control oil in the Middle East. Accordingly, the newspaper equated the United States with the imperialist colonial masters and called for a reasonable Arab solution to Iraq's invasion of Kuwait.

By emphasizing the importance of the control of oil as an economic value and responsibility of the Arab Nation to control oil, the *Times* places special value on Arabs to solve inter-Arab problems through negotiation and dialogue. The *Times* also calls for de-escalation and reasonable accommodation in solving the problem of Iraq invading Kuwait. These values emphasize the positive in the Arab value system. But the United States represents negative values in its aggressive, selfish, hasty, and narrow approach to solving, what the *Jordan Times* insists, is an inter-Arab problem.

Islamic values are not mentioned as such in the editorials, but can be discerned in the continued call by the *Times* for negotiation, development, and community within the Arab Nation. The sheikhdoms are also accused of selling out to the United States in oil deals and also by letting the United States establish troops on Arab soil. Resources in Islam are to be shared within an Islamic community that should not be bound by nationalism or royal leaders. In this context, the *Times'* discussion of economics and oil can be seen to contain a reflection of Islamic values.

The newspaper's insistence on linkage of the Palestinian issue to Saddam Hussein's invasion of Kuwait provided a discussion of what the *Jordan Times* considered the most important issue facing the Arab Nation. Dialogue was, thus, proposed as a way to solve both the Palestinian/Israeli issue and the inter-Arab problem of Iraq invading Kuwait. In either case, the solution lay in a peaceful Arab solution that would protect regional economic and territorial values.

Arab unity emerged in the editorials as the ultimate value. Arab unity would, accordingly, allow Arab nations to settle Iraq invading Kuwait from the perspective of an inter-Arab problem that should be addressed as a political and economic issue. Furthermore, Arabs were advised by the *Times,* to be responsible for the control of oil in the region, and, in doing so keep the imperialist colonial masters (U.S.) out of the Arab Nation's business. And finally, the editorials stressed the importance of addressing the Palestinian issue through a dialogue that would promote unity, development, democracy, and modernization in the Arab Nation.

Non-Arab Newspapers, the Kayhan International and the Jerusalem Post

Analysis of the two non-Arab newspapers, the *Kayhan International* and the *Jerusalem Post,* revealed little similarities in the value systems. Differences can, not only be attributed to religious, geopolitical, and governmental differences, but also to the fact that each newspaper's role within the war narrative differed. Therefore, in discussing the invasion of Kuwait by Iraq, the *Kayhan International* saw itself as an experienced mediator, which could evaluate the situation without being the victim or aggressor. The *Jerusalem Post,* on the other hand, approached the discussion from the perspective of the threatened victim from the very beginning of the crisis. Each newspaper, however, presented its argument in a logical and rational manner that validated its standing as a highly rated newspaper.

The *Kayhan International* presented a logical and rational discussion of Iraq's invasion of Kuwait through four value clusters. Values in the *Kayhan International* centered around religion, Middle East autonomy, economy, and of alliances and oaths.

Religious values originating in Islam and the Muslim's duty to create a just, equitable society through the concept of ummah by which a believer follows laws and rules, both civil and private, and ultimately joins in a community with God, is just one of the Islamic values that predominated the editorials. Also the Koranic concepts of adl and ahsan (balance and compassion), ilm (knowledge), and sabr (patience) appeared as values in the discussion of Middle East autonomy, economy, and alliances.

Islam is, in all aspects, the governing force in Iran. The revolution that ousted the Shah in 1979 was a popular cry for the nation to create an equitable society through Islam. Thus, civil and private issues are governed according to precepts and laws given in the Koran toward all matters concerning Iran and its people.

Middle East autonomy, as a value, called for balance and dialogue in solving what the *Kayhan International* considered regional problems. The United States is, thus seen, as an interventionist nation which is only interested in obtaining its objectives as quickly as possible at the expense of regional nations. The United States is seen as the aggressor, which, by tricking other Middle East members into doing its dirty work (encouraging Iraq in the Iran-Iraq war, using the greedy sheikhdoms to control oil) has proposed the real threat to Middle East autonomy.

This threat is wrapped up in both the U.S. fear of an Islamic republic in Iran (the reason Iraq was financed to fight Iran), but also in its interest to control oil in the region. Thus, oil, and its control, is discussed as an important economic value. This discussion brought out what the *Kayhan International* considered the threat that the United States presented to Middle East autonomy and security, but also revealed how Middle East sheikhdoms (Saudi Arabia, U.A.E., and particularly Kuwait) had sold their Islamic brothers and themselves out to the United States. In this context, Iraq was seen as a victim of not only its own policies, but also of U.S. greed.

Through a discussion of alliances and oaths, the value of laws and rules became apparent. These values stem from, not only Islamic, but, also, tribal traditions which place particular importance on "a man's word" being honored. The United States was again seen as a trickster which quickly sacrificed honorable negotiation based on logic and rationality for its own selfish interests in the Middle East. Throughout the dialogue, the *Kayhan International* placed special value upon Iran's experience with both the United States and Iraq. This experience gave Iran a special understanding of the need for Middle East autonomy and the need for Middle East regional members to solve their problems(especially oil and Iraq invading Kuwait)as a security issue for the region.

The *Jerusalem Post,* on the other hand, took the role of the victim throughout the time period. From a value stance of justifying force and military strength in defense of the Jewish State, the newspaper proceeded to demonize Saddam Hussein as a Hitler-type dictator who was threatening the sovereignty of Israel. Independence, self-reliance, pragmatism, realism, and experience were values that the *Jerusalem Post* considered most important in solving the problem of Saddam Hussein invading Kuwait. Force and military strength were, therefore, considered positive values, while negotiation and dialogue were regarded as weaknesses and thus, negative values. Democracy emerged in the editorials as the only effective form of government with Israel the only true democracy in the region. Consequently, Israel became the experienced victim which, not only understood the tyranny of the Hitler like Saddam Hussein, but also was threatened, misunderstood and blamed by the Middle East nations.

The *Jerusalem Post* found it necessary to devalue Arab unity through a discussion of geopolitical values. This discussion devalued Arabs, especially the PLO and the sheikhdoms as dictatorships which were not responsible enough to handle the acquisition of weapons, the control of oil, or religious matters.

The value that the *Jerusalem Post* put on the survival of the Jewish State of Israel was also apparent in the newspaper's insistence that the Palestinian/Israeli territorial issue was a matter of defense and security for Israel within a regional perspective. Accordingly, the PLO was said to be a terrorist ally of Saddam Hussein and that the survival of the Jewish State depended upon a forceful defense of Israeli territorial rights.

Chapter V
CONCLUSION

This study was designed to deal with reactions and postures of the six conflict zone newspapers during the Persian Gulf crisis through interpretive techniques. Editorials were examined in an effort to understand the perceptions of various issues as they were presented and explained in the newspapers from a number of countries.

The study of the editorials in the conflict zone provided a vehicle to examine and understand issues that are important from a regional, yet multinational and pluralistic perspective. Analysis revealed the roles various national, organizational, and individual actors played in the war narrative. Themes and values were also identified in an effort to understand the various cultural perspectives from which a nation dealt with the war.

This study sought to answer four questions: Who were the major participants during the pre-war and war period for each newspaper? What themes emerge concerning these actors? What values are denoted within the context of various themes showing cultural and socioeconomic relationships within a nation? Are there values that apply to the whole region?

The findings of the study revealed a varied set of participants, themes, and values in the editorials in the conflict zone. However, analysis also reveals certain commonalities and differences of themes and values based upon which one can see certain clusters emerge.

The common themes of Arab-unity and Arabs-divided dominated the editorials in the *Jordan Times* and the *Syria Times*. Both newspapers considered Iraq's invasion of Kuwait to be an inter-Arab problem that should be solved through Arab solidarity and dialogue. Each newspaper saw the United States as the aggressor which, through interventionist policies, was trying to further its interests in the region. However, while the *Jordan Times* saw Iraq as the peacemaker, the *Syria Times* saw it as a bothersome aggressor which was working against the interest of the Intifada, the Arab issue of the highest significance in the region. Neither newspaper demonized Saddam Hussein, nor wanted anything except an Arab solution to Iraq's invasion of Kuwait. However, while the *Jordan Times* maintained a firm and unwavering stance that included incorporating the Palestinian conflict into the overall solution of the problem, the *Syria Times,* stressed the importance of turning Arab attention back to the Intifada, but eventually relented to the international community's pressure and supported allied forces to get Iraq out of Kuwait.

The common themes of Arab-unity, world-unity-and-responsibility, and Saddam Hussein-as-aggressor/Hitler were found in the *Arab News* (Saudi Arabia) and the *UAE News* (United Arab Emirates). Major actors were also similar. The Arab Nation was seen as a victim and as a major player, while Saudi Arabia and the United Arab Emirates were seen as potential victims. Iraq and Saddam Hussein were demonized and brought to the world's attention. The world community was represented by the United Nations, and the United States emerged as the defender and enforcer of the world consensus. They opined that Iraq had violated not only Arab values, it also threatened the stability of the world community. Israel, while mentioned as benefiting from the world's attention being turned to Iraq's invasion of Kuwait rather than the Intifada, was not discussed at great length.

The Kayhan International (Iran), a non-Arab newspaper, attempted to analyze the crisis in-depth, with a logical explanation of the various factors at work, from an Iranian point of view. The *Kayhan International* also took a regional approach and saw Iran as a potential mediator and peacemaker in dealing with the invasion of Kuwait by Iraq. The United States was seen, by the newspaper, as the aggressor upon, not only Iraq, but the entire region. Iraq, which had just finished a long and brutal war with Iran, was considered, not only an aggressor, but also a victim of U.S. manipulation. The sheikhdoms emerged as allies of the United States and, therefore, enemies to their own Arab cause, the Israeli/Palestinian conflict.

The *Jerusalem Post* (Israel) approached the invasion of Kuwait by Iraq as a direct threat to Israel. In its editorials, the *Post* portrayed Israel as a country misunderstood within, not only a regional context, but within a larger international context. Saddam Hussein was demonized as a dictator comparable to Hitler by the newspaper, and the world community was held responsible for protecting Israel from, the Iraqi threat.

Approaching the newspapers from a regional perspective, it becomes apparent that Saddam Hussein was demonized in three newspapers and not in three others. The *Arab News* (Saudi Arabia), the *UAE News* (United Arab Emirates), and the *Jerusalem Post* (Israel), represented nations that were considered allies of the United States and understandably demonized Saddam. Even though the *Jordan Times,* the *Syria Times,* and the *Kayhan International* believed Saddam was misguided, they did not overtly demonize him. The demonization on the part of the other three newspapers was clearly necessary in order to justify the United Nations and United States involvement in the crisis.

Also, a discussion of the control of oil and oil prices was noticeably absent in the *Arab News* and the *UAE News,* while it was discussed openly in the *Jordan Times,* the *Syria Times,* which supported an Arab solution, and the *Kayhan International,* which supported a regional solution to the problem. At the same time the sheikhdoms of Saudi Arabia, the United Arab Emirates, and Kuwait emerged as morally weak Arab nations, which through their alliance with the United States and their misuse of oil money had opened the region to interventionist policies from the West.

In the six newspapers, clusters of values emerge within the context of cultural and socioeconomic relationships. The *Jordan Times* and the *Syria Times* have certain value clusters in common. The values in the *Jordan Times* may be identified under two clusters, Arab unity and economic values. In the *Syria Times,* values are clustered around Arab unity and the defense of the Arab homeland. Apparently the newspaper is preoccupied with the issue of Israeli territorial expansion into the Arab lands, and, therefore, unlike the *Jordan Times,* the newspaper does not devote the same attention and prominence to economic values.

The *Arab News* and the *UAE News,* on the other hand, share the value of Arab unity, but also value the monarchy, and are willing to turn the defense of Arab sheikhdoms over to the world community. Thus, these newspapers value an absolute monarchy, world unity, and the defense of Arabs through force as a way to deal with the problem of Saddam Hussein's invasion of Kuwait.

The other two non-Arab newspapers, the *Kayhan International* and the *Jerusalem Post,* contain distinctly different value clusters. The values in *Kayhan International* (Iran) may be clustered as religious, Middle Eastern autonomy, economic, and alliances and oaths. The invasion problem is approached as a regional problem where the value of Middle Eastern autonomy is discussed by placing importance on Islamic and economic values, and the value of alliances and oaths in reaching a solution.

The *Jerusalem Post* views every issue or problem in its editorials against the overriding value of the right of the Jewish State to exist. Toward this goal, the value of independence and self-reliance dominates the editorials with values denoting geopolitical concerns and the newspaper's desire to separate Saddam Hussein's invasion of Kuwait from any linkage to the Palestinian conflict. The value clusters may be related to independence and self-reliance, geopolitics, and no link.

Arab unity is the fundamental Arab value that is important to all the newspapers in the study, yet the approach is different with each newspaper. The *Syria Times* and the *Jordan Times* believe that Iraq's invasion of Kuwait is an inter-Arab problem that should be solved through Arab unity and solidarity. Both newspapers are prepared to uphold Arab unity even when an Arab solution required the exclusion of the West. The Gulf States newspapers, the *Arab News* and the *United Arab Emirates News,* have a different perception of the dangers that they faced. Because they share a political culture with Kuwait that placed particular value on the monarchy and an affluence based on the production of oil, they ostensibly felt vulnerable to Saddam's possible aggressive designs. Saddam Hussein, therefore, represented an evil power and had to be blamed for destroying Arab unity, the assumed primary value to all Arabs. This fractious situation could only be solved through the West as Saddam Hussein became a threat to not only Arab unity, but the international community. The *Kayhan International,* on the other hand, discusses Arab unity as a negative value. Arab unity, therefore, should not be upheld at the cost of Islamic unity which is inclusive of all Muslims in the ummah. The *Kayhan International* sees an ironic justice in the Kuwaiti sheikhdom being invaded by Iraq, and points out that the sheikhdoms provided various forms of support to Iraq when it had invaded the fellow Muslim, but non-Arab state, Iran under the misguided notion of Arab unity.

And finally, the *Jerusalem Post* derides the whole notion of Arab unity as utopian nonsense that has never existed. Perhaps it also takes comfort in the notion that Arab Unity does not exist, otherwise the threat to its primary value, the survival of the Jewish State, would be much greater. Thus, there is a conflict of interest between Arab unity and the sovereignty of the Jewish State of Israel.

The study also examines the formalistic values reflected in the editorials by discussing the rhetorical practices of each newspaper and the methods of argumentation used. The two non-Arab newspapers, the *Kayhan International* and the *Jerusalem Post* demonstrate a high degree of sophistication in developing their editorial arguments in a logical and rational analysis of the relevant issues and problems. The *Jordan Times* stylistically is superior to all the other Arab newspapers insofar as it presents issues in a relatively unemotional manner. The *UAE News* appeals to its readers through frequent use of hyperbole and emotional language. The *Syria Times* lacked in consistency in the use of English. The *Arab News* uses screaming headlines, given to hyperbole, that indicate a preference for martial language.

Recommendations for Further Studies

Whatever importance and usefulness this study may have is derived from the fact that it has shown the complexity of dealing with regional perceptions in the Middle East. This study has also shown that newspapers will approach the subject of war within the region from the perspective of the role each nation plays in the war scenario.

While this study has sought to answer questions pertaining to various nations in the region and, therefore, contribute to a better understanding of the Middle East, it becomes apparent that many factors contribute to the dynamics of the region. Clearly, this study has contributed to an understanding of the complex nature of the region as discussed in newspapers representing six nations during a particularly stressful time in the region.

Editorials in newspapers during wartime has been studied in the past to determine the techniques of persuasion used to present arguments that tend to justify or deny the nation's participation in the war narrative. In order to better understand a more complete picture of what was going on in the Middle East, other newspaper editorials should be added to a future study. An analysis of an Iraqi newspaper's editorials would add considerably to a more balanced understanding of the war narrative. Despite the best efforts of the researcher it was not possible to obtain representative newspapers from Iraq or Egypt. Also, a study involving analysis of Arab newspaper editorials in some north African countries, such as, Libya, and Morocco would place the study in a more expanded Arab arena.

And finally, a comparative study using editorials from U.S. newspapers would provide a better understanding of where the United States saw itself in the war in comparison to Middle Eastern newspapers' perspective of where the United States stood in the Persian Gulf War.

BIBLIOGRAPHY

Brennan, R. M. G., & Hahn, D.F. (1990). *Listening for a president: A citizen's campaign methodology.* Praeger: New York.

Brown, M.W. (1937). "American public opinion and events leading to World War", *Journalism Quarterly*, 14, 23-34.

Canham, E. D. (1943). "The newspaper's obligation in wartime," *Journalism Quarterly*, 20, 315-317.

Davison, P. (1952). "The role of research in political warfare," *Journalism Quarterly*, 29, 18-30.

Dewey, D.O. (1967). "America and Russia, 1939-41: The views of the New York Times," *Journalism Quarterly*, 44, 62-70.

Emery, E. (1971). "The press in the Vietnam quagmire," *Journalism Quarterly*, 48, 619-626.

Frondizi, R. (1963). *What is value?* LaSalle, IL: Open Court Publishing.

Funkhouser, G.R. (1973). "The issues of the sixties: An exploratory study in the dynamics of public opinion," *Public Opinion Quarterly*, 37, 62-75.

Gannet Foundation. (1991). *The media at war: The press and the Persian Gulf conflict.* Edited by Craig LaMay, Martha FitzSimon, and Jean Sahadi. A Gannett Foundation Media Center at Columbia University: New York.

Gans, H. J. (1980). *Deciding what's news: A study of CBS evening news, NBC evening news, Newsweek and Time.* Vintage Books: New York.

Hyman, H., & Sheatsley, P. (1947). "Some reasons why information campaigns fail," *Public Opinion Quarterly*, 11, 412-23.

Kuhn, T.S. (1970). *The structure of scientific revolutions* (2nd ed.). University of Chicago Press: Chicago, Illinois.

Lasswell, H. D. (1935). "Research on the distribution of symbol specialists," *Journalism Quarterly*, 12. 146-156.

Lasswell, H. D. (1948). "The structure and function of communication in society," In L. Bryson (Ed.), *The communication of ideas.* New York: Institute for Religious and Social Studies.

Lasswell, H. D. (1958). *Politics: who gets what, when, how.* New York: Meridian Books.

Lippmann, W. (1922). *Public Opinion.* Harcourt Brace: New York.

MacDougall, C. D. (1942). "How to read a newspaper in wartime," *Journalism Quarterly*, 19, 40-46.

McCombs, M.E., & Shaw, D. L. (1972). "The agenda-setting function of mass media," *Public Opinion Quarterly*, 36, 176-187.

Rokeach, M. (1968). *Beliefs, attitudes and values.* Free Press: New York.

Schillinger, E. H. (1964). "British and U.S. newspaper coverage of the Bolshevik Revolution," *Journalism Quarterly*, 43, 10-16.

Schudson, M. (1982). "The Politics of narrative form: The emergence of news conventions in print and television," *Daedalus*, 11, 97-112.

Shipman, J.M. (1983). "New York Time's coverage of the war in El Salvador," *Journalism Quarterly*, 60, 719-722.

Sillars, M.O. (1991). *Messages, meanings, and culture: Approaches to communication criticism.* Harper Collins Publishers: New York.

van Dijk, T. A. (1988). *News as discourse.* Lawrence Erlbaum Associates, Publishers: Hillsdale, New Jersey.

Welch, S. (1972). *The American press and Indochina, in Communications in international politics*, Richard L. Merritt (Ed.). University of Illinois Press: Urbana, Chicago, London.

Zaremba, A.J. (1988). *Mass communication and international politics: A case study of press reactions to the 1973 Arab-Israeli War.* Sheffield Publishing Company: Salem, Wisconsin.

INDEX

ABC, 10

Asahi Evening News, 8-9

Al-Aqsa, mosque killings, 23, 28-29, 35-36, 46-48, 78, 84, 99; *see also* Temple Mount in Jerusalem

Al-Assad, President Hafez: as peacemaker, 28, 30, 77; equals Hitler, 48

Al-Sabah monarchy, 40, 84-85

Al-Saud monarchy: as pawns of Washington, 55; as suppressor of Muslims, 56

Algiers Agreement (1975), 78

Aqaba, port on Red Sea, 75

Arab, territorial integrity, 90

Arab-Israeli War, 8-9

Arab League, 72

Arab Nation: as victim, 30; divided, 47; doomed, 52

Arab News (Saudi Arabia): themes and actors, 31-38; Arab unity, 21-23; World unity, 23-24; Saddam Hussein-as-aggressor/Hitler, 24,25; no-linkage, 25-26; summary, 64-66

Arab News (Saudi Arabia): values, 82-89; Arab unity, 82-84; absolute monarchy, 85; world unity, 85-86; formalistic, 87; summary, 108-110

Arab Unity, threatened, 48, 72; a call for, 64; dialogue and compromise, 74

Bolshevik Revolution, 2

Brown, W.M., 2-3

Bush, President George: personal crusade, 22; irrational, 15, 16, 24, 25; incubator story, 24; as strong leader, 33, 86, 88; peace through force, 87; enforcer of world opinion, 42, 92; urged to take strong stand, 49; as des-

perate individual, 53, 103; as
hypocrite, 54; as trickster, 105

Cairo Summit, 35, 40, 83
Canham, E. D., 4
casualties, 4, 5
chemical weapons: use of, 44, 73,
    97
Chicago Tribune, 6
CNN, 10
Craxi, Beltino, 22

Daily Graphic, 8-9
Davison, P., 2
Dewey, D. O., 4-5

El Salvador, 7-8
embargo, 33, 35, *see* sanctions
Emery, E., 5-6

Fahd, King (S.A.), 83
force, justified, 53, 97; peace
    through, 92, 97
foreign troops, buildup of, 78; as
    evil transgressors, 79; as impe-
    rialistic threat, 81; justified, 84,
    86

Gannett Foundation Report, 9-11
Gans, H. J., 15
Gaza Strip, 28
Golan Heights, 30
Gorbachev, President Mikhael,
    33, 35

Hayakawa's trichotomy, 7
Helsinki Summit, 35, 40, 45, 48,
    86, 92, 99
"hostages," 33, 41, 92
Hussein, King of Jordan: as
    peacemaker, 19, 20; calls for
    Arab solution, 74
Hussein, President Saddam (Iraq):
    challenges Israel, 18; linkage
    19; July 4, 1990 speech to
    Arab League, 19, 73; as strong
    Arab, 20, 21, 22; demonized,
    21, 32-33, 41, 92; as cornered
    Arab, 21-22; as peacemaker,
    23, 57; free oil to third world,
    24; weakens Arab cause, 29; as
    Hitler/dictator, 32, 34-35, 41,
    84, 95-96; as enemy of Arabs,
    32; as bad Arab, 83, 91; as rea-
    sonable leader, 72; as defender
    of Arabs, 72; as desperate indi-
    vidual, 86; as evil threat to Ar-
    abs, 87, 88; as enemy of Iraqi
    people, 88

Ibadet (acts of devotion), 101
Intifada, 98
Iran, as peacemaker, 104
Iraq: violates Kuwait, 32; as ag-
    gressor, 41; as enemy of Arab
    Nation, 79; as strong Arab
    shield, 89; as invader, 91; vio-
    lates international law, 92;
    weak, 93
Islamic principles, 101, 102
Israel: enemy of Arabs, 28; bene-
    fits, 28, 52-53; as victim, 61,

96; as enemy of Islam, 78; as
enemy of Arab Nation, 80
Israeli/Palestinian issue, 36, 39,
49, 61, 73

Jerusalem Post: themes and actors, 43-51; Saddam as
Hitler/aggressor, 44-45; world
against Israel, 45-46; friends
and enemies of Israel, 46-47;
more to the friends and enemies of Israel, 47-49; double
standard, 49-50; summary, 66-
69
Jerusalem Post: values, 94-100;
independence and self-reliance,
95-96; geopolitical, 96-98; no-
linkage, 98-99; formalistic, 99-
100; summary, 113-116
Jewish state, survival of, 94
Jordan: as victim, 20, 21; port of
Aqaba, 20, 21; as peacemaker,
73
Jordan Times: themes and actors,
17-27; Arab unity, 18-19; Arabs divided, 20-22; Arabs divided (U.S. and Israel), 22-23;
Saddam Hussein as peace-
maker, 23-26; summary, 62-64
Jordan Times: values, 71-76;
Arab unity, 72-74; economic,
74-76; formalistic, 76; summary, 110-113

Kayhan International (Iran):
themes and actors, 51-59; invasion and U.S. aggressor, 51-54;

compliance, 54-55; Iran as
peacemaker and mediator, 55-
56; Iraq as peacemaker, 56-57;
summary, 66-69
Kayhan International: values,
100-107; religious, 101-103;
Middle East autonomy, 103-
104; economic, 104-105; formalistic, 106-107; summary,
113-116
Khomeine, Ayatollah, 101
Kurds, betrayal by West, 49; as
refugees in Iran, 55

MacDougall, C.D., 3
Moscow News, 8-9

NATO, 33
NBC, 10
New York Times, 4-9
North-South (Arabs), 20, 24, 29,
74

oil, 52, 54, 57, 72, 73, 86, 95, 96,
104

Palestinian/Israeli issue, *see* Is-
raeli/Palestinian issue
"Palestinizing of Kuwait," 49
Persian empire, 104
PLO, 46, 47, 95, 98, 99
"Reagan speak," 54, 106

Safer, Morley, 5

Salisbury, Harrison, 5
Sanctions, 33, 35, Jordan suffers,
    75
San Francisco Chronicle, 6
Saudi Arabia: as victim, 23, 25;
    monarchy attacked, 54-55
Schillinger, E. H., 2
Shari'a (law), 101
sheikhdoms, as greedy dictator-
    ships, 97; control oil, 104
Shipman, J.M., 7-8
Soviet Union, 8 point peace plan,
    25
Straits Times, 8-9
Syria, as peacemaker, 28
Syria Times: themes and actors,
    27-31; Arab unity and Arabs
    divided, 27-30; summary, 62-
    64
Syria Times: values, 77-82; Arab
    unity, 77-78; Arab homeland,
    78-80; formalistic, 80-81; sum-
    mary, 110-113

technology, 4, 11
Times of London, 8-9

Ummah (unity through commu-
    nity), 83
United Arab Emirates News:
    themes and actors, 38-43; Arab
    unity, 39, international-com-
    munity as peacemaker, 40;
    Saddam as greedy-aggressor,
    41-42; summary, 64-66
United Arab Emirates News: val-
    ues, 89-94; Arab unity, 89-92;

    defense of Arabs through
    force, 92-94; formalistic, 93-
    94; summary, 108-110
United Nations, embargo, 20, re-
    sponsible for solution, 32-33,
    40, *see* embargo and sanctions
United States; equals Israel, 19,
    22-23; double standard, 19, 28,
    29; oil interests, 19, 20, 25; as
    aggressor, 20-23, 52, 61; as in-
    terventionist, 21, 29, 61, 72;
    presence in Middle East, 32; as
    powerful force, 45; placates
    Arabs, 46; as hypocrite, 52; as
    enforcer, 62; as alley of Israel,
    73; divides Arabs, 73; arming
    Israel, 80; as leader, 96

van Dijk, Teun A., 14-15
Viet Nam, 1, 5-7, 10

Wall Street Journal, 7-8
Washington Post, 6
Welch, S., 6-7
world unity, 40
WWI, 3
WWII, 3-5

Zaremba, Alan Jay, 8-9
Zayed, Sheikh, 39, 90